TODAY in
HISTORY

GW00471264

Disney

Eve Zibart

books

For further information, contact the publisher at:

Emmis Books
1700 Madison Road
Cincinnati, OH 45206
www.emmisbooks.com

Library of Congress Cataloging-in-Publication Data
Zibart, Eve.
    Today in history: Disney/by Eve Zibart.
        p. cm.—(Today in history series)
    ISBN-13: 978-1-57860-276-6
    ISBN-10: 1-57860-276-9
    1.Walt Disney Company—Calendars. 2. Walt Disney Company—
History—20th century. 3. Walt Disney Company—History—
21st century. I. Title. II. Series.
    PN1999.W3Z53 2005
    384'.8'0979494—dc22
                                        2005019086

Cover and interior designed by Carie Adams
Production design by Annie Long
Edited by Lady Vowell Smith

Distributed by Publishers Group West

INTRODUCTION

This calendar is an offshoot of a much larger project involving fairly extensive research, in the course of which I not only rediscovered many of my own favorite Disney attractions, I also became familiar with a whole cast of amazingly talented and astoundingly versatile people, not just Walt Disney himself but his collaborators and employees reaching back to the very beginning of the studios. None of them were specialists—and I mean that as a huge compliment. They were artists, animators, inventors, writers, musicians, singers, dancers, sculptors, puppeteers, comedians, jokesters, pranksters, tinkerers, technicians, special-effects and sound wizards, most of them self-taught and more than a few among the first and best teachers of the next generation of animation professionals. No wonder Walt had to coin a new word—*Imagineering*, a combination of *imagination* and *engineering*—to refer to that brilliant and indefatigable crew. Walt may have been the visionary, but hundreds of hands and hearts and minds were involved in the evolution of Walt Disney Studios. Although most of their stories did not make it into this volume, these eclectic geniuses entertained and educated me day after day.

Even today, the Disney Company is in the hands of brilliant, funny, and endlessly curious professionals. Disney's theme parks have been widely imitated, but the peculiarly fantastic, romantic, and even idealistic underpinnings and backstories have never been equaled. And the studio's partnership with Pixar, itself greatly indebted to Disney and the Disney-sponsored CalArts training, has reinvigorated the art of animation for yet another generation.

And so, in recognition not only of their own impressive bodies of work but of their contributions to that amazing world of imagineering, this book is dedicated in part to Marty Sklar and Joe Rohde.

It is also dedicated to the scores of Disney historians and fans, professional and amateur, whose passion and scholarship fill Web sites and fanzines around the world. First among them is Dave Smith, who created the Disney archives and has written a number of magazine articles and columns in addition to *Disney A to Z* and other books. Patiently and kindly, Smith served as the final authority on disputed dates and titles. Walt Disney World media specialists Rick Sylvain and his staff also supplied much-appreciated assistance.

Thanks also to Molly Merkle and Lady Vowell Smith, who held their breath right up until press time; Len Testa, a great "flying" partner; and my husband, Don Tippman, the best research assistant anyone could have.

—*Eve Zibart*

january

Disney Magic, *Walt Disney Co.'s first cruise ship, arrives at Port Canaveral, Florida, 1998, from Italy, where she was built.*

1

January

(1888) Walt Disney's parents, Elias Disney and Flora Call, were married in Akron, Florida. The two met in Ellis, Kansas, and when the Calls relocated to Florida, Elias trailed along, bought a citrus plantation, and married their daughter. In 1889 he took a job as a building contractor in Chicago, where Walt was born. In 1906, Elias moved the family to Marceline, Missouri, and tried to make a go of a farm.

Elias was never lucky in any business he tried, and he stayed on the move until Walt and his brother Roy brought their parents to Hollywood years later. Tragically, Flora died when the furnace in their home malfunctioned in 1938. Elias Disney died in 1941.

BY THE NUMBERS

Disneyland grossed more than $10 million in its first year.

DISNEY QUIZ

What onetime Disney animator became only the second student accepted into Disney's animation studies program at the California Institute of the Arts in the mid-1970s?

John Lasseter, Oscar-winning writer and director of *Toy Story*

(1938) *The Mickey Mouse Theater of the Air,* sponsored by Pepsodent toothpaste, debuted on NBC Radio. The series—seven programs of a half hour each—continued until May 15. The programs (which are still available on tape) are especially precious because they feature most of the original character voices: Walt Disney as Mickey, Clarence "Ducky" Nash as Donald Duck, and Pinto Colvig as Goofy, as well as Hal Reese doing sound effects and Felix Mills and his orchestra providing live music.

January

DID YOU KNOW?

After the end of the 1964–65 New York World's Fair, for which Walt Disney created four attractions, New York planner and World's Fair president Robert Moses asked Walt Disney to turn the fairgrounds into an East Coast Disneyland. Disney politely declined.

3

January

(2005) London-based lorry driver Nick Pain told the *Sun* newspaper that he was naming his newborn son Walt Disney. "I've loved the films since I was a little boy and still enjoy them," explained Pain, 40, of Fordingbridge, Hants. Pain, who already sported a tattoo of Snow White and the seven dwarfs across his back, said he hoped a little of the Disney magic might rub off on the 7-pound, 3-ounce future moviegoer. "Walt Disney brought joy to millions, and I hope my son has as magical a life as the characters in his films."

DID YOU KNOW? ————————

When animators Frank Thomas and Milt Kahl first showed Walt Disney the rough scenes from *Bambi* in which a butterfly lands on Bambi's tail and Bambi trips over a log on top of Thumper, Disney's eyes welled up. "Fellas," he said, "this is pure gold."

DISNEY QUIZ ————————

In what original *Wonderful World of Disney* movie did Ronald Reagan Jr. make a cameo appearance as a White House security guard?

My Date with the President's Daughter (1998)

(1936) "Mickey's Polo Team," the 80th cartoon starring Mickey Mouse, was released. "Polo" portrayed Walt's round-eared alter ego as the captain of a team of Disney characters—including, oddly, the Big Bad Wolf, in one of the few times he and Mickey play nicely—that takes on a rival team featuring many recognizable Hollywood celebrities, such as Charlie Chaplin, Harpo Marx, Laurel and Hardy, and Will Rogers. Many of the horses resemble their riders: Laurel's is thin, Hardy's is rounder, and Marx is pictured riding an ostrich.

4
January

NAME THAT 'TOON

What Disney short was rushed into production and finished in only three months so it could be the opening feature for *The Pride of the Yankees*, Samuel Goldwyn's biopic about New York Yankees star Lou Gehrig?

"How To Play Baseball" (1942), the first of the "How To" cartoons featuring Goofy

5

January

(2004) In a reverse tribute, Matt Groening's *The Simpsons* visited a Florida theme park called EFCOT. This was only one of the show's many Disney references—generally in the sly, insult style typical of the cartoon. One *Simpsons* segment titled "Two Dozen and One Greyhounds" includes a song called "See My Vest" (think "Be Our Guest" from *Beauty and the Beast*). A dream sequence parodying "Under the Sea" from *The Little Mermaid* has Homer Simpson eating all the seafood—in other words, Ariel's companions. The evil Mr. Burns shares pasta, à la *Lady and the Tramp*, with his beloved. And the musical show called "Simpsoncalifragilisticexpiali-D'oh-cious" needs no explanation.

WHERE'S MICKEY?

Mickey Mouse was the first cartoon character ever to be awarded a star along Hollywood's Walk of Fame, at 6925 Hollywood Boulevard on November 18, 1978, in honor of his 50th anniversary.

(1963) "Three Tall Tales," which brought together three of Disney's most popular cartoon featurettes, "Casey at the Bat," "Paul Bunyan," and "The Saga of Windwagon Smith," aired on *Walt Disney's Wonderful World of Color*. By way of introduction, Walt explains about the extravagant tall tales of Baron Munchausen; then Ludwig von Drake takes over to introduce the three segments. "Paul Bunyan," originally released in 1958, was nominated for an Oscar in the category for Best Cartoon Short.

January

DID YOU KNOW?

"There's a Great Big Beautiful Tomorrow," the song the Sherman brothers wrote for the Carousel of Progress at the New York World's Fair, was one of Walt's favorites. When the carousel moved to Walt Disney World in 1975, the song was changed to "The Best Time of Your Life," but complaints were so persistent that the song was changed back when the ride was renovated in 1993.

BY THE NUMBERS

One bit of trivia has it that the 26,000 feet of lights strung about the re-created geographical landmarks in *IllumiNations*, Epcot's signature fireworks show, would reach across the Golden Gate Bridge six times.

7

January

(**1931**) The black-and-white short *The Birthday Party* was released, but apparently it aged quickly, because a decade later it was remade in color as *Mickey's Birthday Party*. The two shorts have almost identical plots: Horace Horsecollar, Clara Cluck, and Clarabelle Cow throw Mickey a surprise party at Minnie's house. The most obvious difference in the versions is the way Mickey and Minnie are drawn. In the earlier short, both still have pointed, upturned noses and ears that are fully circular and side-by-side no matter from what angle the character is seen. By the later film, their faces and bodies are rounder and their costumes are no longer limited to shorts and skirt.

DID YOU KNOW?

A small coonskin cap on the logo for Fess Parker's critically acclaimed winery in Santa Barbara pays tribute to Disney's *Davy Crockett* series in which Parker starred in the 1950s.

8

January

(1981) Gert Schelvis was announced as the 200 millionth visitor to Disneyland. Exactly 23 years later, on January 8, 2004, that record was eclipsed when Bill Trow of Wentworth Falls, Australia, became the 500 millionth visitor.

After Disneyland opened, it took less than two months for the park to register its millionth visitor and less than six years to welcome 25 million. Yet attendance at the much larger Walt Disney World has grown twice as fast. It reached the 50 million mark in less than five years and 100 million in eight years. Its 600 millionth guest was singled out on June 24, 1998.

DISNEY QUIZ

Disney's Golden Oak Ranch in California, where such movies as *The Apple Dumpling Gang*, *Pete's Dragon*, and *The Muppet Movie* were filmed, has also served as the filming location for commercials for what popular restaurant chain?

Kentucky Fried Chicken

9

January

(1937) *Don Donald*, the second film to be released with the dashing duck in the starring role, made clear that Donald could carry a series without help from Mickey. Donald had first appeared as a supporting character in one of the "Silly Symphony" films, *The Wise Little Hen*. The irascible and often unintelligible Donald caught on immediately, and by 1961 he had starred in 128 cartoons, a syndicated daily comic strip, and a series of comic books.

BY THE NUMBERS

It is estimated that nearly 20,000 weddings have been performed at Walt Disney World alone, at a rate of 2,300 weddings a year and at a minimum cost, for a weekend date, of $10,000.

(1930) Roy Edward Disney, only child of Roy O. and Edna Disney, was born. His long, turbulent career with the company his father and uncle founded—he resigned twice and engineered one coup to hire Michael Eisner and another to fire him—would split both the family and the company into bitter camps. Roy E. grew up among the animators and went to work for the studios in 1954. As head of the animation department in the late 1980s, he is often credited with such successes as *The Lion King* and *Beauty and the Beast.* In a surprise ceremony on October 16, 1998, Eisner named him a Disney Legend.

10
January

LEGENDARY PEOPLE

What Goofy voice-over expert would go on to clown around as the beloved Bozo, on record albums, at live appearances, and on a regular TV show?

Pinto Colvig, named a Disney Legend in 1993

11
January

(1929) The very first meeting of the very first Mickey Mouse Club chapter was called to order, precisely at noon, at the Fox Dome Theater in Ocean Park, California. Theater manager Harry Woodin had the idea of making the Saturday matinees into gathering places for kids, and the concept was quickly adopted by hundreds of theaters around the country. By 1932, there were more than a million club members nationwide; and the allegiance they felt to their clubs laid the groundwork for *The Mickey Mouse Club* of television a quarter century later.

DISNEY QUIZ

In 1965, the more technical areas of Walt Disney Imagineering were spun off into a division called MAPO. The meaning of the acronym has since been changed to "manufacturing and production organization." What was it originally taken from?

Mary Poppins, the phenomenally successful film released in 1964

12

January

(1936) The *New York Times* quoted author H. G. Wells as calling Walt Disney a "genius." "All Hollywood studios are so busy that they keep very much to themselves," Wells said. "Consequently, Chaplin never visited the Disney studios. Imagine, Chaplin and Walt Disney, those two geniuses, never met! I took Charlie there. Disney has the most marvelous machinery and does the most interesting experiments." It's appropriate that Wells refers to Disney's machinery and experimentation, since the author wrote such influential science-fiction books as *The Time Machine*. Wells himself appears in Walt Disney World's *The Timekeeper*, portrayed by Jeremy Irons.

DID YOU KNOW?

In 1997, *Life* magazine included Walt Disney on its list of the 100 most influential people of the millennium. Walt came in at number 90. The list's top ten started with Thomas Edison at number one, followed by Christopher Columbus, Martin Luther, Galileo Galilei, Leonardo da Vinci, Isaac Newton, Ferdinand Magellan, Louis Pasteur, Thomas Jefferson, and Joseph Stalin.

13

January

(1930) The first Mickey Mouse comic strip ever published appeared in the *New York Mirror*, in a syndicated deal with King Features. Walt Disney wrote the story, which was a loose adaptation of the script for *Plane Crazy*, and Ub Iwerks, who had animated that film two years earlier, naturally drew it. Iwerks was succeeded by his assistant, Win Smith, who drew the strips for three months. In May, Floyd Gottfredson took over, also supposedly as an interim assignment, but he remained to draw the strip for 45 years, right up until his retirement.

"Walt is no mouse. . . . Because Walt can seem shy and retiring with people he doesn't know well, and because Roy has been heard to complain that Walt has no more money sense than Mickey Mouse, the myth has grown up that Mickey Mouse is a projection of Walt's real personality. I can assure you it isn't true. No matter how hard the rest of us squeak, Walt goes ahead and does what he wants to do."

—Lillian Disney

14

January

(1977) *The New Mickey Mouse Club,* the second of three separate series and, like the proverbial middle child, the one often overlooked, premiered on ABC. It aired until December 1, 1978. The show was caught in a time of cultural change. Unlike the original, it was in color, although color television was certainly no novelty by the late 1970s. This series had a dozen new Mouseketeers who were supposed to attract a more contemporary, hipper audience, although only one, Lisa Whelchel, who later played Blair on *The Facts of Life,* went on to have much of a career. Either the cast or the concept never quite clicked with the children of the 1960s, and the show was canceled after only two years.

NAME THAT 'TOON

In what cartoon does Pluto's singing turn off the lady dogs so much that he lip-syncs "You Belong to My Heart" from *The Three Caballeros?*

"Pluto's Blue Note" (1947)

15
January

(1975) When the Space Mountain attraction was officially unveiled at Walt Disney World, it had a real guest star as its first "astronaut": Col. James Irwin, who had piloted the lunar module of the *Apollo XV* mission. The first computer-controlled thrill ride, Space Mountain remains a favorite attraction. The ride's popularity is due in part to its unpredictability: the roller coaster travels in the dark, while passing comets and shooting stars distract the eye. Ray Bradbury, the eminent science-fiction writer, reportedly consulted on the design.

DID YOU KNOW?

On New Year's Day in 1966, Walt Disney presided over the Tournament of Roses Parade in Pasadena, California, as grand marshal. He rode through the crowd in an open white Cadillac with Mickey Mouse at his side.

16

January

(1994) The inaugural Walt Disney World Marathon was held, drawing a field of 8,500 runners. In 1998, a half-marathon was added, along with a wheelchair division. In 2004, the 11th annual run drew a record 24,000 participants: 15,500 for the full circuit and 8,500 for the 13-mile race.

One of the marathon's greatest assets, aside from its being in good-weather territory during winter, is that the route runs through all four theme parks and sometimes offers a little glimpse of future attractions or backstage magic. Certainly there are few other races where you might have Mickey Mouse cheering you on.

DISNEY QUIZ

In 2004, what became the tallest float in the Tournament of Roses Parade history?

Disneyland's Tower of Terror–inspired float called "Sudden Drop in Pitch," which featured a 100-foot-tall tower

17
January

(2003) A live stage version of *Aladdin* called *Disney's Aladdin: A Musical Spectacular* opened at the Hyperion Theater in Disneyland at Anaheim. It was one of several Disney productions that, following the *Beauty and the Beast* and *Lion King* models, borrowed mainstream theatrical talents to reshape established franchises. *Disney's Aladdin* was directed by Francesca Zambello, who has directed musicals and operas for the Royal National Theatre and Royal Opera at Covent Garden in London, and it was choreographed by Lynne Taylor-Corbett of *Footloose* and the Tony-winning shows *Titanic* and *Swing!*

BY THE NUMBERS

In doing detailed field research for the film *Aladdin*, the advance team took more than 1,800 photographs of the city of Esfahan, Iran, alone.

DID YOU KNOW?

Whenever asked, Walt Disney would finesse the question of whether Mickey Mouse and Minnie were married by comparing them to such famous on- and off-screen couples as Mary Pickford and Douglas Fairbanks.

(1999) *So Weird*, a series about a rock star and her kids who encounter paranormal phenomena while traveling the country in a bus, premiered on the Disney Channel. Described as a cross between *The Partridge Family* and *The X-Files*, this show featured a widowed mom named Molly Phillips, played by Mackenzie Phillips, onetime star of *One Day at a Time* and daughter of singer John Phillips.

18
January

(2002) The Disney movie *Snow Dogs* premiered. Starring Cuba Gooding Jr. as a Miami dentist who inherits a team of crack sled dogs, it has a typical Disney plot: boy meets dogs and girl, boy gets dumped by dogs and girl, boy gets dogs and girl.

DISNEY QUIZ

What famous Disney movie tune does the foghorn of the cruise ship *Disney Magic* play?

"When You Wish upon a Star"

19
January

(1949) *So Dear to My Heart,* one of Disney's earliest classic family films about a young boy and his lamb, was released. Based on the novel *Midnight and Jeremiah,* by Sterling North, *So Dear to My Heart* stars the two children from *Song of the South,* Bobby Driscoll and Luana Patten. Driscoll, as Jeremiah Kincaid, lives on his grandmother's farm, where he adopts a black lamb as his pet. Arguably the high point of Driscoll's career, *So Dear to My Heart* was one of the films that earned the 12-year-old a special Oscar for outstanding juvenile actor that year.

DISNEY QUIZ

What is Minnie Mouse's full name?

According to a 1942 comic strip story, her name is actually Minerva.

January

(2005) The peak of "Mount Everest," site of the Expedition: Everest thrill ride in Walt Disney World's Animal Kingdom, was lowered into place. It tops out at just short of 200 feet—about one-fiftieth the size of the real Everest. This pet project of Imagineering vice president Joe Rohde, who directed the construction of the entire Animal Kingdom theme park, cost Disney $100 million by the time it opened. During research for the attraction, Rohde repeatedly led designers, architects, and storytellers through Nepal and Bhutan—flying, hiking, canoeing, and riding donkeys.

DID YOU KNOW?

Marceline, Missouri, the small town where Walt Disney spent much of his childhood, has become the ideal hometown of many Americans, thanks to Walt's re-creations of it as Main Street and in such movies as *Summer Magic* and *Pollyanna*.

21
January

(1933) *The Mad Doctor*, a Mickey Mouse spoof on classic horror films and one of the studio's best early shorts, was released. It is one of at least three Disney shorts making reference to the classic Frankenstein movies. Tim Burton's 1984 *Frankenweenie*, which also involves the monsterization of a dog, uses actual props from the Boris Karloff version. And in the 1995 *Runaway Brain*, Mickey's brain is transplanted into a monster's body by Dr. Frankenollie, a tribute to animating team Frank Thomas and Ollie Johnston.

DISNEY QUIZ

How did legendary actor **Walter Brennan**, who played in three Disney films between 1965 and 1968, acquire his distinctively high, hoarse voice?

Assigned to an artillery unit in World War I, he was exposed to poison gas that ruined his vocal cords.

NAME THAT 'TOON

What cartoon shows Goofy not only participating in an animated history of the evolution of sailing and demonstrating methods of navigation, but also defeating the Japanese navy?

"How To Be a Sailor," released amid the growing war fever of 1944

January

(1984) Walt Disney Productions staged the halftime show for Super Bowl XVIII in Tampa Bay, titled "Salute to the Superstars of the Silver Screen." The final game score was Los Angeles 38, Washington 9.

Disney has provided halftime entertainment at a number of Super Bowl games: Super Bowl XI in 1977; Super Bowl XXI in 1987; Super Bowl XXV in 1991; Super Bowl XXIX in 1995, with Tony Bennett and Patti LaBelle; and Super Bowl XXXIV in 2000, featuring Phil Collins, former Mouseketeer Christina Aguilera, and Enrique Iglesias. The theme for both the 1977 and 1991 shows was "It's a Small World." Apparently the line gets stuck even in Disney's memory.

LEGENDARY PEOPLE

Who played the jolly lead in *The Santa Clause* and *The Santa Clause 2* and provided the commanding voice of Buzz Lightyear in both *Toy Story* movies and the Buzz Lightyear's Space Ranger Spin rides at Walt Disney World in Orlando and Tokyo Disneyland?

Tim Allen, named a Disney Legend in 1999

23

January

(1942) *The New Spirit*, a propaganda short commissioned by the U.S. Treasury Department, was delivered after only four weeks' production. The story features Donald Duck as an ordinary guy who is reluctant to pay his income taxes. But then, hearing over the radio how important it is to win the war—"Taxes defeat the Axis"—he races to Washington to deliver his payment in person as Cliff Edwards, later the voice of Jiminy Cricket, sings "Yankee Doodle Spirit." Seen by 60 million Americans, the film was so successful that a sequel was requested. *The New Spirit* was even nominated for the Best Documentary Academy Award.

DID YOU KNOW?

Russi Taylor, longtime voice of Minnie Mouse, also provides the voices of several recurring characters on the hit show *The Simpsons*, including Bart's friend Martin, the twins Sherrie and Terri, Uter the exchange student, and Uter's mother.

(1993) *Aladdin,* the highest-grossing (more than $500 million) animated film of its time and an ideal showcase for the whizbang, catch-the-punch-line-if-you-can, stream-of-consciousness style of Robin Williams as the Genie, picked up its first two major awards: the Golden Globes for Best Score and Best Song. Plus, a special award went to Williams for his voice-over. The awards, given by the Hollywood Foreign Press Association, are considered good indicators for the Academy Awards, and in this case, they were. The movie would go on to win four Grammy Awards on March 1 and two Oscars on March 29.

24
January

DISNEY QUIZ

Who served as the model for the original Tinker Bell in the 1953 *Peter Pan?*

Though many believed the character was modeled on Marilyn Monroe, Tinker Bell was based on former *Our Gang* child star Margaret Kerry. Then 22, she had won the title "Most Beautiful Legs in Hollywood," and said she snagged the role by ad-libbing the scene in which Tink looks in a mirror, surveys her ample shape, and stamps her feet in annoyance.

January

(1961) *101 Dalmatians,* one of Disney's best and most successful films, premiered. Instead of inkers tracing every drawing by hand, this movie was the first to use Xerox copiers to transfer all the animators' drawings onto celluloid, which saved a huge amount of time and money—and probably several artists' eyesight, considering the millions of Dalmatian spots that would have had to be traced. Even with this money-saving innovation, the film cost $4 million.

DISNEY QUIZ

In the Rock 'n' Roller Coaster Starring Aerosmith attraction, what is found on the license plates of the five limos that transport thrill seekers?

UGOGIRL, 1OKLIMO, 2FAST4U, H8TRAFFC, and BUHBYE

LEGENDARY PEOPLE

What composer received Oscar nominations for the scores of the Disney movies *Cinderella, Snow White and the Seven Dwarfs,* and *Song of the South* and won an Oscar for the score of *Pinocchio,* including the famous song "When You Wish upon a Star"?

Paul J. Smith III, named a Disney Legend in 1994

(1958) Comedian Ellen DeGeneres, who came out as a lesbian on television in 1997, was born in New Orleans. According to overnight Nielsen ratings, the April 30, 1997, episode of *Ellen* drew an audience of 42 million Americans. "The Puppy Episode," as it was known, was the last straw for the 15 million–member Southern Baptist Convention, which one year earlier had given the Disney Company a year to clean up its controversial corporate policies; on June 18, they voted to boycott Disney, ABC, the theme parks, and Disney-related outlets. But Disney and *Ellen* had the last laugh: five months after the boycott was announced, company stock went up 10%, and the show's ratings hit an all-time high.

26
January

NAME THAT 'TOON

In what early Disney cartoon did Donald Duck do a brief Jimmy Durante impersonation, saying, in Durante's trademark staccato, "Am I mortified"?

The 1934 "Orphan's Benefit" (though, for whatever reason, the bit was edited out when the cartoon was rereleased in 1941)

January

(2004) Former directors Roy E. Disney and Stanley Gold, who had launched a campaign to have CEO Michael Eisner removed, sent a letter to company shareholders in advance of the annual meeting. Their letter began, "Now is the time for all Disney shareholders to take the first step to bring needed change to The Walt Disney Company. . . . Just by saying NO you will send a message the Board of Directors cannot ignore." The battle between Eisner and Gold and Disney had recently led to Disney's being forced off the board and Gold's subsequent resignation in protest. The increasingly strident campaign set the stage for a showdown at the shareholders' meeting in Philadelphia in March 2005.

DISNEY QUIZ ———————————————

Who was the first to "take the controls" of the Mission to Mars attraction when it opened at Disneyland in Anaheim in 1975?

Astronaut Story Musgrave

(1999) The Montreal-based Cirque du Soleil took up permanent residence in a specially constructed theater at Disney World. *La Nouba,* the name of the Disney show, originates from the French phrase *faire la nouba,* which means "to party" or "to live it up." The troupe's publicity calls the show "the story of all stories, the site of all mysteries, where dreams and nightmares sleep side by side." And, echoing Walt Disney's own phrase about his theme parks, the description says, "Here, anything is possible."

28
January

"Disneyland will never be completed. It will continue to grow as long as there is imagination left in the world."

—*Walt Disney*

NAME THAT 'TOON

What Oscar-winning war short shows Donald Duck suffering the humiliation of having to "Heil!" Hitler?

"Der Fuehrer's Face" (1943)

29
January

(1920) Eighteen-year-old Walt Disney went to work at Kansas City Slide Company, which became Kansas City Film Ad. They made commercials, crude stop-action shorts using cardboard characters, that were shown in movie houses. Once he had mastered the technique, Disney borrowed a camera and experimented with a reel of short cartoon-strip gags and then sold them to a local cinema. That was the beginning of the Newman Laugh-O-Gram shorts. Within two years, Walt had enough money to turn the Laugh-O-Grams into his own company.

(1987) Snow White and all seven dwarfs rang the closing bell at the New York Stock Exchange, in celebration of the Disney Company's highest-ever fourth-quarter earnings.

NAME THAT 'TOON

Long before Elton John wrote "The Circle of Life" for *The Lion King,* what other Disney movie took the cycle of the seasons and the constant chain of life and death as its themes?

Bambi

(1988) *IllumiNations*, Epcot's signature fireworks show, debuted at Walt Disney World, replacing the older *Laserphonic Fantasy*. The show was revamped, updated, and up-teched first in 1996, in time for Disney World's 25th anniversary, and then again in October 1999 as part of the great millennium celebration, when it was called *IllumiNations 2000: Reflections of Earth*. It now features curved LED television screens, a 150,000-note score, and 1,500 pyrotechnic effects that require 67 computers in 40 different locations.

30
January

DISNEY QUIZ

Who christened the cruise ship *Disney Wonder* when it was launched in August 1999?

Tinker Bell, using a laser beam instead of the traditional bottle of Champagne

DID YOU KNOW?

Local chapters of the Mickey Mouse Club, founded in 1929, met in theaters around the country, elected officers (a chief Mickey and a chief Minnie), recited Scout-style pledges, and then watched Mickey Mouse cartoons together.

31
January

(1978) Two of Disney's Nine Old Men, the nickname Walt Disney gave his core group of animators in the 1950s, retired together, as best friends should. Frank Thomas, who joined Disney in 1934 as an assistant animator, and Ollie Johnston, who started in 1935 as an "in-betweener" on Mickey Mouse cartoons, worked on most of the major animated features from _Snow White_ to _The Fox and the Hound_. Thomas's best-known sequences include Bambi on the ice and the spaghetti-sharing moment between Lady and Tramp. Johnston not only contributed to two dozen films but often served as directing animator as well.

DISNEY QUIZ

What is the only film for which "Retlaw Yensid" (Walt Disney spelled backward) received a writing credit?

Lt. Robin Crusoe, U.S.N. (1966)

LEGENDARY PEOPLE

What American sweetheart and _Beach Party_ movie star was discovered by Walt Disney himself, who made her into one of the most memorable Mouseketeers of all time?

Annette Funicello, named a Disney Legend in 1992

February

Dick Van Dyke dances outside a Hollywood, California, theater on the night of the world premier of the Disney film Mary Poppins, *1965. At left is costar Julie Andrews; at right is Walt Disney.*

1

February

(1989) Disney CEO Michael Eisner announced the formation of Hollywood Pictures, to take part of the production burden off Touchstone Pictures and to serve as a vehicle for more adult-interest films. The new logo's first release, in 1990, was *Arachnophobia,* a retro sci-fi thriller about an infestation of poisonous South American spiders in California. Hollywood Pictures' biggest hits included *The Joy Luck Club, Quiz Show,* and *Mr. Holland's Opus.* Most of its films were only middlingly successful, however; and in 1998, the company merged with the Touchstone and Disney studios to become the Buena Vista Motion Pictures Group.

BY THE NUMBERS ————————————

The "inspection certificate" for the elevators at *The Twilight Zone* Tower of Terror is numbered 10259—or, 10/2/59, the date that Rod Serling's influential television show, *The Twilight Zone,* premiered.

(1967) Roy Disney held a press conference to announce plans for EPCOT Center, as it was then known. The high point of the conference was a videotape that Walt had recorded the previous October, before he passed away in December.

2
February

Standing for Experimental Prototype Community of Tomorrow, EPCOT was intended to be a city with a commercial hub, radiating suburbs, and first-class educational, medical, and service facilities. It actually evolved into something more like an elaborate world's fair. The closest thing to Walt's vision are the Future World pavilions, which explore technology designed to improve people's quality of life.

DID YOU KNOW? ————————

The name of Steve Martin's character in the *Father of the Bride* movies is George Stanley Banks, a tribute to two earlier movies: the father in *Mary Poppins* is George Banks, while in the original *Father of the Bride*, Spencer Tracy plays Stanley Banks.

LEGENDARY PEOPLE ————————

What star of the 1961 film *The Absent-Minded Professor* became the very first Disney Legend?

Fred MacMurray, named a Disney Legend in 1987

3

February

(1945) The popular *Three Caballeros* cartoon was released, following a special world premiere in Mexico City on December 21, 1944. Like its 1942 predecessor, *Saludos Amigos*, it was a collection of four shorts set in Latin America and partly inspired by a goodwill visit Walt Disney made to South America in 1941. In its entirety, the exhilarating film starring Donald Duck seems somewhat like a tequila fantasy, studded with bits of wild dancing and lively music.

DISNEY QUIZ ————————————————

Which of the seven dwarfs were based on real Hollywood personalities?

According to Disney animators, Sleepy was described as Sterling Holloway, and Dopey—a name that some staffers worried sounded too modern and alluded to narcotic addiction, but that Walt claimed to have found in Shakespeare—was based on vaudeville comedian Eddie Cantor.

(1966) The first Winnie-the-Pooh feature, *Winnie the Pooh and the Honey Tree,* was released. Its sequel, *Winnie the Pooh and the Blustery Day,* came out after Walt Disney's death but had been approved by him beforehand. Based on the hugely popular books by British author A. A. Milne, and featuring such endearing characters as Owl, Eeyore, Kanga, and Roo, *Honey Tree* would be followed by numerous full-length and short-format features, animated television series, and even educational films, not to mention theme park attractions. The most recent full-length Pooh film, *The Heffalump Movie,* came out in February 2005.

4
February

DID YOU KNOW?

Ward Kimball, one of Disney's most important animators, held various part-time jobs as a teenager working his way through art school in Santa Barbara, California, in the early 1930s. One at the Fox Arlington Theater involved conducting the ten-piece band that opened the Mickey Mouse Club meeting every Saturday. By 1934, at the age of 20, Kimball had become an apprentice animator at the company.

5
February

(1953) *Peter Pan,* one of Disney's most enduring films, premiered at the Roxy Theatre in New York City. In 1939 Walt Disney received permission to make the film from the Great Ormond Street Hospital in London, to whom *Peter Pan* author James M. Barrie had bequeathed the rights. Production did not begin until 1949.

The swaggering story of the fearless boy who learns to fly and runs away to live with the fairies, the Indians, and the pirates captivated audiences. Many have remarked that Walt may have felt a special kinship with the boy who refused to grow up.

DID YOU KNOW? ─────────

In the Mission: Space attraction at Disney World, the images of the planets were computer-generated from real satellite and spacecraft data.

DISNEY QUIZ ─────────

What sport did Walt, Roy, and other Disney employees play in their spare time?

Polo. They used to practice twice a week in the San Fernando Valley, beginning early enough that they were all at the studio by the usual 8 a.m.

(1934) Marty Sklar, the company's most influential creative presence after Walt Disney himself, was born in Long Beach, California. Sklar is one of the last to work closely with Walt—so closely that he has been nicknamed "The Sorcerer's Apprentice." "When Marty says something is good, it's almost like Walt says it's good," Imagineering president Don Goodman once remarked.

6
February

As head of WED, Sklar oversaw the design, construction, and expansion of theme parks on three continents as well as the cruise line and merchandise stores. He is also credited with Epcot's creation. Since 1996, Sklar has been titled vice-chairman and principal creative executive of Walt Disney Imagineering.

BY THE NUMBERS

The budget for the 1953 Disney classic *Peter Pan* nearly reached $4 million, in part because filmmakers first shot a live-action version of many scenes in order to give the animators a more intense vision.

7

February

(1940) *Pinocchio*—the film many critics consider Walt Disney's greatest achievement, both artistically and technically—debuted at the Central Theater in New York City. It was the first feature to make full use of the multiplane camera, which was extremely expensive to operate but allowed for a more realistic three-dimensional look, a look that was further sharpened by the extensive use of puppet and live-action models. No matter how widely acclaimed it was, the film was not a box office success, probably because with the outbreak of war in Europe, it seemed too dark and forbidding—despite its happy ending.

DISNEY QUIZ ————

How did Disney World celebrate the Rock 'n' Roller Coaster Starring Aerosmith attraction's first anniversary in 2000?

By parking 80 Corvettes in the shape of the attraction's guitar logo

NAME THAT 'TOON————

What Disney film re-creates a moment early in Walt and Lilly Disney's married life, when Walt surprised his wife with a puppy inside a hatbox as a Christmas gift?

Lady and the Tramp

(2001) Disney's California Adventure, a 55-acre park built over Disneyland's parking lot in Anaheim, officially opened. At that time, California Adventure boasted three districts: Golden State, a celebration of California's cultural diversity and natural beauty; Hollywood Pictures Back Lot, a paean to the bygone glitz of moviemaking; and Paradise Pier, a salute to traditional Pacific Coast amusement parks. A fourth district, A Bug's Land, with the 3-D "It's Tough To Be a Bug!" attraction, opened in 2002.

Despite huge advance publicity, California Adventure had a small debut. Staffers estimated the opening-day audience would number around 33,000 people; by noon, only about 14,000 tickets had been sold.

8
February

WHERE'S MICKEY? —————————

Author and critic John Updike once called Mickey Mouse "the most persistent and pervasive figment of American popular culture in the [twentieth] century."

9

February

(1996) The Disney Institute, CEO Michael Eisner's concept of a modern Chautauqua, opened to the public. A combination of summer camp and adult education campus, the institute offered 60 courses in performing arts, cooking and entertaining, gardening, sports and health, computer skills, financial management, and even such Disney specialties as Claymation, computer animation, and sound mixing. In addition, the institute boasted two performing arts venues, a cinema, and a spa. Unfortunately, the idea didn't take off as Eisner had hoped. The institute closed in 2003, and after extensive renovation, it reopened in 2004 as the Saratoga Springs Resort.

DID YOU KNOW? —————————————

Lisa Whelchel, who played Blair on *The Facts of Life,* started as a Mouseketeer on *The New Mickey Mouse Club* in 1977–78. She was one of the only reasonably successful actors to emerge from the second of the three *Mickey Mouse Club* series.

(1951) Robert A. Iger, who would become president of the ABC network and then, after the Walt Disney Company purchased ABC, climb the Disney ladder to president and then CEO, was born in New York. He became notable for his ability to navigate the treacherous shoals of Disney corporate politics.

10
February

Iger was named president and chief operating officer of the Walt Disney Company in January 2000. Two years later, he was chosen to succeed Michael Eisner as CEO, taking charge on October 1, 2005. Iger brought much-needed stability to the Disney upper ranks in a time of falling revenues and increasing internal acrimony. In the three years before his arrival, Disney had gone through one president and two studio heads, two chief financial officers, and three ABC network chiefs.

LEGENDARY PEOPLE

Who was the only American actor in the cast of the Disney movie *Mary Poppins?*

Dick Van Dyke, named a Disney Legend in 1998

11
February

(2004) Comcast announced it would attempt a hostile takeover of the Walt Disney Company, and the proposed merger became a hot topic in the media. Disney stock prices immediately jumped 15%, and the Dow Jones closed at its highest point in three and a half years. Such a merger would have created what the *Wall Street Journal* called "a media behemoth." Comcast initially proposed to buy Disney for about $54 billion in Comcast shares and assume nearly $12 billion in Disney debt. The attempt was averted, though it added to the pressure on CEO Michael Eisner to improve earnings.

DID YOU KNOW? ————————————————

Mission: Space has the distinction of being the first Disney attraction with motion sickness bags as standard equipment. So many riders became ill either blasting off or free-floating that the bags were added within the first few months.

NAME THAT 'TOON ————————————————

Which animated Disney classic did film critic Roger Ebert include in his book *The Great Movies?*

(1809) Abraham Lincoln was born in Harlan County, Kentucky. More than a century and a half later, thanks to Disney Imagineering, the assassinated president would rise from the grave to address his "fellow Americans" again in the Great Moments with Mr. Lincoln attraction at the New York World's Fair. Lincoln became the first audio-animatronic "human," and one of Disney's most famous technological marvels.

12
February

Now, at Walt Disney World in Orlando, Lincoln appears among all his presidential peers, though he still sits front and center and, in an echo of his original performance, rises from his chair when introduced.

DISNEY QUIZ

What beloved animated animal almost made the cover of *Time* magazine?

Dumbo the elephant was scheduled to be *Time* magazine's cover boy in December 1941, two months after the movie's premiere. However, after the attack on Pearl Harbor, Japanese admiral Isoroku Yamamoto got the spotlight.

13

February

(1996) The GM Test Track Preview Center, designed to increase interest in the planned high-speed attraction, opened in Epcot at Walt Disney World. Disney World promised the thrill ride would be open the next May. However, while construction went smoothly, vehicle technology continued to be tricky. The cars' wheels consistently succumbed to the rigors of the ride, and the computerized operating systems kept crashing. Finally, on March 17, 1999, Disney celebrated Test Track's grand opening, presided over by NASCAR hero Richard Petty and supermodels Christie Brinkley, Angie Everhart, Frederique, and Carol Alt. Test Track's waiting lines continue to be among the longest at Walt Disney World.

BY THE NUMBERS —————————————

According to Disney archivist Dave Smith, the 1940 film *Pinocchio* required the talents of 750 artists, 2 million drawings, and some 1,500 shades of paint.

(1969) The Singing Busts of the Haunted Mansion went into the studio to record "Grim Grinning Ghosts," the attraction's theme song. The singers, which included Thurl Ravenscroft, were also the models for the busts. The busts were created from photos taken at the session, and a week later the singers came back to be filmed. Ravenscroft said he was startled when he saw the film effect: "One minute it's just a dead bust, and the next there I am in the flesh and blood and I can see my tongue and the inside of my mouth and my teeth. You know, it was frightening!"

14
February

DISNEY QUIZ

Who invented the Disney Mousegetar, a four-string "tenor guitar" turned into a toy version that Mattel marketed in the late 1950s?

Mickey Mouse Club host Jimmie Dodd

"Mickey was my first introduction to humor and comedy. He was the good guy."

—Dick Van Dyke

15

February

(1950) *Cinderella,* one of Disney's most successful features and its first full-length cartoon since *Bambi,* was released. This film represented another high-stakes gamble, and if it had failed, the studios might have, too; but this time Disney hit gold. With its glossy storybook look, *Cinderella* was full of romance and classic Disney humor. Some of its most effective characters are actually animals: think of the mice Gus and Jaq (both voiced by Jim MacDonald, by then the voice of Mickey Mouse). And while some characters seem completely real—Cinderella, her prince, her stepmother—the duke, the king, and the stepsisters remain cartoons.

DISNEY QUIZ

Who made a lasting contribution to Disney fandom by designing the Mickey Mouse Club ears?

Roy Williams, cohost of the original *Mickey Mouse Club*

NAME THAT 'TOON

What is the only animated feature in Disney history to have been rated PG rather than G?

The Black Cauldron (1985)

(1904) James Baskett, the first actor hired by Walt Disney for a full-length film, *Song of the South,* was born. Not only did Baskett play Uncle Remus, he also provided the voice for Brer Fox and filled in on Brer Rabbit in the "Laughing Place" sequence. As Uncle Remus, he sang "Zip-a-Dee-Doo-Dah," which took the Oscar for Best Song. And in 1948 he received a special Oscar "For his able and heart-warming characterization of Uncle Remus, friend and story teller to the children of the world." This made him the first (live) actor in a Disney film to be recognized by the Academy of Motion Picture Arts and Sciences. Baskett died only three months later.

16
February

DID YOU KNOW?

In 1983, when Sally Ride returned from the mission that made her the first woman astronaut in space, she was asked about the sensation. Ride, a native of Southern California, described it as "a real E-ticket ride." Until 1982, Disneyland used ticket books of varying prices, called A tickets, B tickets, and so on, as admission to simpler (A and B) or more elaborate (C and D) attractions. The top attractions required E tickets, so Ride was saying that space had lived up to her childhood fantasies.

17

February

(2004) The Walt Disney Company announced that it would acquire rights to puppeteer Jim Henson's Muppets and Bear in the Big Blue House properties—the characters, films and television library, and all associated trademarks—for what industry analysts estimated at $60 million plus some share in royalties. In addition, the companies signed a four-year agreement to develop new movie and television programs. The Muppets had already appeared in several Disney films, including *The Muppet Christmas Carol,* and a couple of TV specials. In addition, they starred in *Jim Henson's Muppet Vision 4-D* shows at Walt Disney World and Disney's California Adventure.

DISNEY QUIZ

What renowned astronomer was asked to weigh in on the birth-of-creation segment set to Stravinsky's "Rite of Spring" in *Fantasia?*

Edwin Hubble, for whom the deep-space telescope is named

(1960) The Winter Olympics in Squaw Valley, California, were officially declared open, with Walt Disney orchestrating both the opening ceremonies and the closing show. The International Olympic Committee turned the fanfare portions of the 1960 Winter Games over to Disney for good reason: these were the first games to be nationally televised, and thus a little more than the traditional torch lighting was needed to impress the audience. Disney obliged. The opening ceremony involved some 5,000 performers, including 52 bands from California and Nevada; fireworks; and the release of 2,000 pigeons impersonating doves.

18
February

"Walt Disney is a thing, an image people have in their minds. And I spent my whole life building it. Walt Disney, the person, isn't that image, necessarily. I drink and I smoke, and there's a whole lot of other things that I do that I don't want to be part of that image."

—Walt Disney

19

February

(1952) Chinese American author Amy Tan was born in Oakland, California. In 1993, Hollywood Pictures would release a film version of her successful debut novel, *The Joy Luck Club*. The book and film are autobiographical, at least in the sense that Tan's real history inspired them. Like the novel, the film focuses on four Chinese women and their daughters. During their weekly mah-jongg games, the mothers complain, console, congratulate, and commiserate about the difficulties of raising their daughters in America. Meanwhile, the daughters struggle to find a balance between their mothers' traditions and values and their own modern outlook.

LEGENDARY PEOPLE

What artist served as head of Disney's comic strip department in the 1940s, overseeing strips starring Donald Duck, Uncle Remus, and "Silly Symphonies" in addition to daily and Sunday Mickey Mouse strips?

Floyd Gottfredson, named a Disney Legend posthumously in 2003

(1904) Clarence "Ducky" Nash was born. Originally a ventriloquist who visited schools and amused children with his animal imitations, Nash dropped by the Disney studios looking for work; but Walt Disney said Nash "sounded like a damn duck." A year later, when Walt had the idea for a salty, Popeye-like duck, he thought of Nash. For a half-century, Nash was the voice of Donald Duck in English and other languages. A *Nation* magazine reporter said he talked "as if he had a larynx full of hot golf balls." After Nash's death in 1985, animator Tony Anselmo took over Donald's vocal chores.

20
February

DISNEY QUIZ

What is distinctive about the Goofy wristwatch, which has been re-created as a classic at Disney stores?

The numbers are listed backwards, and his arms move counterclockwise.

BY THE NUMBERS

At Disney's California Adventure in Disneyland, the 6,000-foot-long California Screamin' is the world's longest steel looping roller coaster. It makes an entire 360-degree loop and goes from zero to 55 mph in four seconds, a rate any race-car driver would envy.

21

February

(2001) At the presentation of the Grammy Awards, the original cast recording of Tim Rice and Elton John's *Aida,* an adaptation of Verdi's 1871 opera, won honors as Best Musical Show Album. At the same show, singer-songwriter Randy Newman won the award for Best Original Song Written for Motion Picture, Television, or Other Visual Media, for "When She Loved Me" from *Toy Story 2.* And, in a tie-in to the same movie, Riders in the Sky won the Grammy for Best Children's Album for *Woody's Roundup.*

NAME THAT 'TOON————————————

What animated classic inspired the design of the Team Disney building (the Walt Disney World corporate headquarters) in Burbank?

Snow White and the Seven Dwarfs. Designed by Michael Graves, the building features a row of bas-relief sculptures of the dwarfs holding up the roof of the building—just as *Snow White* had shored up the studio's financial house back in the 1930s.

(2004) The company announced that it would begin hosting guided tours of Wyoming and Hawaii as tests for expanding its vacation business. Called Adventures by Disney, the 15 prototype tours were limited to 30 people and cost between $6,000 and $8,000 for a family of four. The idea, according to a press release, was to re-create in real-life settings the "immersive family vacation experience that started with Disneyland Park 50 years ago." The Hawaiian itinerary included expeditions to the volcanos, surfing lessons, and a luau, while the Wyoming tour ranged through the Grand Teton and Yellowstone national parks.

February

DISNEY QUIZ

In 2000, what popular TV actor paid more than $30,000 for the metal Disneyland banner, with its distinctive initial "D," which stood over the entrance to the parking lot from 1989 to 1999?

John Stamos. Some accounts say Stamos bought the Disneyland sign because it was the site of his first date with ex-wife supermodel Rebecca Romijn; Stamos has said it was the classic first-date place for Los Angeles boys when he was growing up.

23

February

(1935) Mickey Mouse made his first full-color film appearance, in "The Band Concert." However, it was not quite the end of Mickey's black-and-white career; "Mickey's Kangaroo," the last cartoon to be released in black and white, did not premiere until nearly two months later, on April 13.

(1938) Walt Disney received his famous special Academy Award for *Snow White and the Seven Dwarfs*. Tiny superstar Shirley Temple presented Walt with a specially made Oscar, flanked by seven miniature Oscars.

DISNEY QUIZ ————————————————

Whose 2005 album *Got No Strings* gave new swing to ten classic Disney tunes, including a honky-tonk waltz version of "A Dream Is a Wish (Your Heart Makes)" from *Cinderella* and a bluesy "Spoonful of Sugar" from *Mary Poppins*?

Michelle Shocked

DID YOU KNOW? ————————————————

Walt Disney gave the train station from the 1949 film *So Dear to My Heart* to Imagineer Ward Kimball for his full-size locomotives at home.

(1960) The movie *Kidnapped,* a Robert Louis Stevenson adventure set in Scotland during the Jacobite rebellions, was released. With its harrowing trek through the Highlands, the scenes of cruelty aboard ship, and its theme of friendship between enemies, it should have been a rollicking adventure, but critics found it pedestrian. It was not nearly the success Stevenson's *Treasure Island* had been a decade before.

24
February

Kidnapped was directed by Robert Stevenson, the director of such Disney standards as *Mary Poppins* and *The Love Bug.* Despite the efforts of Hollywood flacks to hype the movie, director Stevenson insisted he was not related to the author.

NAME THAT 'TOON

What 1943 Disney-produced war propaganda film shows, in a powerful climax, an American eagle plunging a dagger into the heart of Japan?

Victory Through Air Power, based on the book by Maj. Alexander P. de Seversky

25

February

(1988) Television aired "Totally Minnie," a special that at long last put Minnie Mouse in the star's chair (and that costarred a blonde as giddy as Minnie herself, Suzanne Somers). The show included clips from Minnie's long film career and a brand-new video in which the mouse costarred with Elton John. Minnie had been receiving her somewhat belated dues since 1986, which became "The Year of Minnie Mouse" at the theme parks. Nearing her 60th birthday, she was honored with a "Totally Minnie" parade at Disneyland, a much-needed wardrobe update, and a new theme song.

BY THE NUMBERS

To replace the original Disneyland parking lot on which Disney's California Adventure was built, the company constructed a garage big enough to hold 10,000 cars—the largest parking structure in the world.

26
February

(1942) Walt Disney was presented the Irving G. Thalberg Award by the Academy of Motion Picture Arts and Sciences. It was just one of the statuettes he had to juggle that night. On behalf of the Disney studios, Walt received two Oscars: a special technical award for "outstanding contribution to the advancement of the use of sound in motion pictures through the production of *Fantasia* and the Best Cartoon Short Oscar for "Lend a Paw." Conductor Leopold Stokowski and his associates got a special Oscar for their "creation of a new form of visualized music" in *Fantasia*, and Frank Churchill and Oliver Wallace won Best Original Score for *Dumbo*.

DISNEY QUIZ

Why did a certain production cel from *101 Dalmatians* sell for a staggering $61,200 during a 2005 auction?

Walt Disney had inscribed the cel to John Kennedy Jr., who was killed in the crash of a private plane he was piloting in 1999. The inscription reads, "To John Jr.—All the best wishes from Walt Disney." The cel was sold as part of two large auctions of Kennedy family memorabilia orchestrated by Caroline Kennedy Schlossberg.

27

February

(1994) Olympic skater and silver medalist Nancy Kerrigan skipped the Lillehammer games' closing ceremonies to head for Orlando and her promotional duties for Disney. Kerrigan, who came in second but garnered national sympathy through a feud with Tonya Harding, made a multimillion-dollar deal with Disney. In addition to starring in a skating video, a TV movie, and more, Kerrigan was supposed to appear in various Disney promotions. But almost immediately, she was caught on camera during a Disney parade saying, "This is the corniest thing I've ever done. I can't believe I'm doing this!"—and except for one 1995 TV special, the contract was canceled.

DISNEY QUIZ

What cruel-hearted Disney movie character has been described— by the character's creator, Marc Davis—as a combination of Bette Davis, Rosalind Russell, and Tallulah Bankhead?

Cruella De Vil in *101 Dalmatians*

28

February

(1994) ABC broadcast a segment of the news-magazine *Day One* charging that Philip Morris "spiked" its cigarettes with extra nicotine to make it harder for smokers to quit (the network later apologized without retracting the charge). It was the first public airing of controversial allegations against the tobacco industry that would eventually earn the *Wall Street Journal* a Pulitzer Prize. The report inspired an in-house battle at CBS over whether to air a Mike Wallace interview with whistle-blower Jeffrey Wigand; a *Vanity Fair* article called "The Man Who Knew Too Much"; and, in 1999, the Touchstone film *The Insider,* which earned seven Academy Award nominations.

DISNEY QUIZ

What is the name of the 1991 musical collection, also released on video, featuring Billy Joel's version of "When You Wish upon a Star," Harry Connick Jr.'s "Bare Necessities," and Bobby McFerrin's scatting of "The Siamese Cat Song"?

Simply Mad about the Mouse

29
February

(2004) Director-screenwriter Andrew Stanton, who had been only the second animator to join the Pixar Animation Studios (after John Lasseter himself), accepted the Best Animated Film Oscar for *Finding Nemo*. Not only did Stanton write the story and screenplay for the hugely popular *Nemo*, but he directed it and supplied the voice for the film's famous Crush the Turtle.

Stanton's voice-overs are a studio in-joke. He has supplied at least one voice in each of the Disney-Pixar films except *Monsters, Inc.* Among his credited voices are Hopper in *A Bug's Life* and Emperor Zurg in *Toy Story 2*.

DID YOU KNOW?

To help himself imagine the yeti, or the abominable snowman, for the Expedition: Everest attraction at Disney World's Animal Kingdom, Imagineer Joe Rohde stocked his office with the skull of a *Gigantopithecus*, a ten-foot primate that became extinct 500,000 years ago.

March

Walt Disney and his family arrive from a three-month trip abroad at Los Angeles, California, 1949. He is posing with his wife, Lillian, and their daughters Diane and Sharon.

1

March

(1999) Two of the most popular attractions at Walt Disney World's Animal Kingdom, the Kali River Rapids ride and the Maharajah Jungle Trek, opened as centerpieces of the Asia section. The Kali River Rapids was the second thrill ride in Animal Kingdom, much less terrifying than Dinosaur! and as popular for its cooling effects as for any supposed suspense. The Maharajah Jungle Trek leads visitors through an old-fashioned aviary, constructed like a giant, tropical-foliage birdcage; bat cliffs; the waterfall home of a Komodo dragon; and a great stone ruin upon which Asian tigers lounge.

DISNEY QUIZ

Who is the unlikely singer of "Someday My Prince Will Come," from *Snow White and the Seven Dwarfs*, on the 1988 Grammy-winning *Stay Awake: Various Interpretations of Music from Vintage Disney Films?*

Sinead O'Connor

BY THE NUMBERS

In the Test Track attraction at Disney World, each vehicle has three onboard computers processing 100 million calculations per second, three times the computing power of the space shuttle; travels at a top speed of 65 mph; and has six braking systems to handle the 22 wheels.

2

March

(1955) Jay Osmond, the youngest of the original Osmond Brothers, was born in Salt Lake City, Utah. Although many people assume the brothers debuted on *The Andy Williams Show*, they signed their first professional contract with Disney and made their first television appearances on Disney specials.

Jay and brothers Alan, Wayne, and Merrill were visiting Disneyland in 1961—all dressed identically—when the Dapper Dans barbershop quartet noticed them and asked if they sang. The two quartets alternated in an impromptu concert. The Osmonds were immediately signed and spent the summer as strolling singers in the park.

LEGENDARY PEOPLE

What vice chairman and principal creative executive of Walt Disney Imagineering said that Walt Disney's death in 1966 "actually affected [him] more than when [his] father died"?

Marty Sklar, named a Disney Legend in 2001

3
March

(2004) Roy E. Disney and Stanley Gold's long, public, and acrimonious campaign to remove Michael Eisner from his position as CEO sparked a populist revolution among shareholders. A letter sent by Disney and Gold urging shareholders to vote against Eisner resulted in an unprecedented 43% no-confidence vote at the shareholders' meeting in Philadelphia. The board voted to strip Eisner of his title as chairman of the board, and the directors promised to search for a new CEO. In September, Eisner announced that he would retire on September 30, 2006. In March 2005, Disney president Robert Iger was chosen to succeed Eisner.

DISNEY QUIZ

Where did Pleasure Island, the nightlife entertainment park at Walt Disney World in Orlando, get its name?

Pinocchio, which depicts a land of infinite fun that lures Pinocchio and his friends and lets them indulge in anything they like, until they turn into donkeys

(1914) Ward Kimball, one of the most important of Walt Disney's Nine Old Men, was born. Kimball was hired as an in-between in 1934 and within five years had become one of Disney's premiere animators. He was a mainstay of *Fantasia* (particularly Bacchus and his donkey), *Pinocchio* (primarily Jiminy Cricket), and *Dumbo*. Despite his lightheartedness, Kimball was also influential in Disney's serious science ventures, including the "Man in Space" series. He created "Toot, Whistle, Plunk and Boom," the first CinemaScope cartoon, in 1953.

4
March

DID YOU KNOW?

Comedian Ellen DeGeneres has a long association with the Disney Company. In 1992, she landed a supporting role in an ABC sitcom called *Laurie Hill* and later went on to headline in her own ABC series, *Ellen*. She and "Science Guy" Bill Nye are the stars at the Universe of Energy pavilion at Epcot, and for a while the bookstore at Disney-MGM Studios was called Ellen's. One of her most popular roles was as the voice of Dory, the forgetful but good-hearted regal blue tang fish in Disney's *Finding Nemo*.

5
March

(1936) A "Silly Symphony" called "Three Orphan Kittens" was named the Best Short Subject Cartoon of 1935. Its use of perspective is remarkable because, while previously backgrounds had been relatively static, some sequences in "Kittens" show the background shifting as the point of view changes. The story focuses on three kittens who are abandoned during a snowstorm and take refuge in a house where they proceed to break dishes, "play" the piano, and wreak havoc on their surroundings.

(1932) Disney released "The Mad Dog," a Mickey Mouse cartoon in which Pluto learns the downside of disobedience.

BY THE NUMBERS ————————————

Even now, 40 years after his death, Walt Disney holds two Academy Award records: he received the most nominations of any artist (59), and he received the most awards as well (32 Oscars, including three special awards as well as the Irving G. Thalberg Award).

(1999) The 37-year-old Swiss Family Treehouse in Disneyland entered its last weekend before being rehabilitated and retitled for a new audience as Tarzan's Treehouse. When the treehouse reopened about three months later, only a few days after the premiere of the animated film that inspired it, much of the general structure remained the same, but instead of the Robinsons' hut at the top of the staircase, the homes belong to Tarzan's dead parents and his foster mother, the ape Kala, as well as Tarzan himself.

March

DISNEY QUIZ

What musician's name made him the perfect choice to perform "When You Wish upon a Star" on the 1988 Grammy-winning *Stay Awake: Various Interpretations of Music from Vintage Disney Films?*

Ringo Starr

NAME THAT 'TOON

What 1929 Mickey Mouse cartoon salutes Al Jolson by combining titles from two of his popular films?

"The Jazz Fool"

7

March

(1942) Michael Eisner, Disney's second-longest-running CEO after Walt Disney himself, was born into a wealthy New York family. On his 20-year watch, the Disney Company would acquire ABC/Cap Cities, buy (and sell) a big-league baseball franchise and an NHL hockey team, launch several successful cable television channels and Touchstone and Hollywood Pictures, buy Miramax Pictures and partner with Pixar, Inc., launch vast new merchandising campaigns, and turn out some of its most successful animated films in history. The CEO would also star in some of the most infamous corporate wrangling in history.

NAME THAT 'TOON

What cartoon spoof on classic horror films has an evil scientist named Dr. XXX dognapping Pluto and carrying him off to a crumbling castle as a subject for his experiments?

"The Mad Doctor" (1933)

DISNEY QUIZ

Why did the Disney Company demand an apology after the Academy Awards show in March 1989?

In the show's opening segment, "Brat Pack" actor Rob Lowe sang "Proud Mary," and danced with a Las Vegas showgirl dressed as the beloved Disney character Snow White. The furious Disney Company received its apology some weeks later.

(1983) President Ronald Reagan, who had been one of the emcees at the grand opening of Disneyland in 1955 and, as a personal friend of Walt Disney, had visited the park repeatedly after that, made his first visit to Walt Disney World in Orlando. Two years later, after single-digit temperatures in Washington, D.C., had forced the cancellation of his second inaugural parade, Reagan presided over a Memorial Day makeup parade at Epcot featuring 21 bands originally scheduled to perform in January. Reagan returned to Disneyland in 1985 and again in 1990 for the celebration of the Anaheim park's 35th birthday.

8
March

"Walt Disney's true drawing table was the imagination. His themes were virtues like courage and hope, and his audience was composed of young persons—in years or in heart—who, through the creations of this American genius, found new ways to laugh, to cry and just plain appreciate 'the simple bare necessities of life.' "

—1986 U.S. Senate resolution making December 5, 1986, which would have been Walt's 85th birthday, a nationwide Walt Disney Recognition Day

9
March

(1955) The *Disneyland* TV show aired "Man in Space," the first of three programs over three years on the future of space travel. It was such a stunning achievement that the next day, President Dwight D. Eisenhower reportedly phoned Walt Disney to congratulate him on the program, and to request a copy of the tape to show Pentagon officials. "Man in Space" used animation to explain the history of rockets, including the ancient art of Chinese fireworks; the problems of weightlessness; and the design of multistage engines.

DID YOU KNOW?

The original model for "EPCOT Center," as it was initially known, can still be seen at Walt Disney World, not in Epcot but at the Magic Kingdom: as the Tomorrowland Transit Authority winds through Space Mountain, the 10- by 20-foot model is visible on the left.

(1938) *The Old Mill* not only continued the studios' nearly unbroken streak of Best Animated Short Subject Oscars but also earned Walt Disney his first scientific and technical Oscar for the development of the multiplane camera. A famously moody and dramatic film almost nine minutes long, *The Old Mill* depicts a storm as it threatens a farmyard mill and the animals who make their home inside. Eventually, of course, the storm passes, the sun returns, and all is well.

10
March

NAME THAT 'TOON

Which animated film marked the first time Mickey was digitally animated, using the technique developed for the Mickey's PhilharMagic attraction?

The made-for-video *Mickey's Twice upon a Christmas*, released in 2004

DISNEY QUIZ

What is former First Lady Nancy Reagan's surprising connection to the Disney movie *Aladdin*?

Some Disney animators have said (mostly off the record) that the face of the evil vizier Jafar was partly based on Nancy, wife of Walt Disney's longtime friend Ronald Reagan.

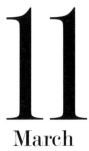

11
March

(1962) *The Prince and the Pauper,* the first version of Mark Twain's classic story the studios would create, premiered as a three-part TV series. It starred Guy Williams, already a Disney star as Zorro, and Disney child-actor regular Sean Scully in the two title roles: Prince Edward VI, son of King Henry VIII, and Tom Canty, the street urchin who so resembles him that he is nearly coronated.

Disney made an animated featurette of *Prince and the Pauper* in 1990, starring Mickey Mouse as both the prince and the urchin who discover they have identical faces.

DISNEY QUIZ

What young actor voiced Beary Barrington in the 2003 feature *The Country Bears?*

Haley Joel Osment

LEGENDARY PEOPLE

What former president of Disneyland created the influential Disney Dollars, inaugurated in March 1987, that guests use to buy Disney merchandise at on-site resorts?

Jack B. Lindquist, named a Disney Legend in 1994

(1928) Though the date is uncertain, on or about this day Walt Disney renounced any further interest in the character of Oswald the Lucky Rabbit, Disney's first successful animated creature. The next day, he wrote a famous telegram to Roy: "LEAVING TONIGHT STOPPING OVER IN KC ARRIVE HOME SUNDAY MORNING SEVEN THIRTY DON'T WORRY EVERYTHING OK WILL GIVE DETAILS WHEN ARRIVE—WALT." Distributor Charles Mintz had shocked Walt by disclosing that Universal Pictures, not the Disney studios, owned the rights to Oswald— which threw Walt into a rage. A few days later on the train, Walt supposedly got the idea for Mickey Mouse.

12
March

DID YOU KNOW?

In a famous mix of live action and animation, the scene in *Mary Poppins* showing Mary, Bert, and the children jumping into Bert's chalk sidewalk drawings was created using a new composite cinematography technique developed by, among others, Ub Iwerks. The technique scored an Oscar the next year.

13
March

(1969) *The Love Bug,* starring Dean Jones, Michele Lee, Buddy Hackett, and Disney regular David Tomlinson, was released. A seemingly simple, almost innocuous film, it would turn out to be the largest-grossing film of the year and eventually spawn three movie sequels, a limited television series, and in 1997 a two-hour TV movie. Then, in June 2005, perhaps inspired by the resurrection of the Volkswagen Bug, the car returned as the pumped-up star of *Herbie: Fully Loaded,* featuring Lindsay Lohan and including such real-life NASCAR superstars as Dale Earnhardt Jr.

"When people laugh at Mickey Mouse, it's because he's so human; and that is the secret of his popularity."

—*Walt Disney*

BY THE NUMBERS ————

The movie *Pinocchio,* released in 1940, cost a staggering $2.6 million to make, which by some estimates would be well over $100 million today.

(1994) The Virginia state legislature approved a package of $163 million in incentives to assist Disney in building its proposed 400-acre American-history theme park, Disney's America, near the Manassas battlefield in Virginia. Disney estimated it would cost $650 million, including 6,000 housing units, 1,300 hotel rooms, a water park, golf courses, and two million square feet of commercial space. The park was supposed to draw six million tourists a year and generate 19,000 jobs for Prince William County, just outside Washington, D.C. But six months later, the project was canceled, thanks to a campaign that focused on the potential impact of heavy traffic, infrastructure pressure, and commercialization on the dozens of historic sites in the area.

14
March

DISNEY QUIZ

In a 2005 poll of actors, musicians, and athletes, which Disney character did the most people identify with?

Goofy, said 20% of the celebrities polled, including John Stamos, Jim Belushi, and Kelsey Grammer. Their opinions were supported by the general public: 15% of 8,000 respondents also selected the affable Goof as the character to whom they most closely relate. (The Disney Company commissioned the poll as part of the 50th anniversary of Disneyland's opening.)

15

March

(1927) Jack B. Lindquist, who started out as the advertising manager for Disneyland and wound up as its president, was born in Chicago. Lindquist joined Disney in 1955 and by 1971 was vice president of marketing for both Disneyland and Walt Disney World. In 1990, he became president of Disneyland, where his colleagues nicknamed him "Honorary Mayor." Lindquist supervised the development of Epcot and Tokyo Disneyland and helped plan Disneyland Paris. His most successful promotional idea may have been to invite children from all over the world to pour water from every ocean into the river of "It's a Small World."

NAME THAT 'TOON

Although Paul J. Smith III usually worked behind the scenes as a composer on such hits as *Pinocchio, Cinderella,* and *Snow White and the Seven Dwarfs,* in what animated feature did he appear on screen?

Fantasia, in which he was a violinist

(1961) *The Absent-Minded Professor,* the first of a series of popular films featuring the space-age Flubber, was released. It would make the giddy goo a buzzword. The movie was nominated for three Oscars, including one for its special effects. Filmed in black and white, it was colorized in 1986 but re-released in black and white in 1993.

16
March

DID YOU KNOW?

Walt Disney personally persuaded 84-year-old actress Jane Darwell, who had won an Oscar playing Henry Fonda's mother in *The Grapes of Wrath* in 1940, to come out of retirement at the Motion Picture Country Home to play the Bird Woman in *Mary Poppins.* It was her last performance.

"Mickey seems to be the average young boy of no particular age; living in a small town, clean-living, fun-loving, bashful around girls, polite and clever as he must be for the particular story. In some pictures he has a touch of Fred Astaire, in others of Charlie Chaplin, and some of Douglas Fairbanks, but in all of these there should be some of the young boy."

—Disney artist Fred Moore, known as the "Mickey expert"

17
March

(1939) After several years as a repertory character, Goofy was confirmed as a full-fledged family member with the release of "Goofy and Wilbur." Despite his long ears and muzzle, Goofy was meant to be a person, like Mickey, as opposed to Pluto, who was a dog. In his initial appearance, in "Mickey's Revue" (1932), Goofy was an unidentified audience member who said nothing but released a distinctive laugh that caught Walt's imagination. The laugh came courtesy of gagman Pinto Colvig, who also gave Goofy his first speaking voice.

DISNEY QUIZ

Who were among the foreign dignitaries who toured Disneyland in its early days?

President Sukarno of Indonesia, King Bhumibol and Queen Sirikit of Thailand, King Mohamed V of Morocco, King Mahendra and Queen Ratna of Nepal, King Baudouin of Belgium, and Indian Prime Minister Jawaharlal Nehru

(1967) The Pirates of the Caribbean attraction, the last ride in which Walt Disney was personally involved, opened in Disneyland. It has been reproduced at the parks around the world and remains one of Disney's most popular rides. It also inspired one of the studios' biggest movie hits in decades. The attraction's extensive use of audio-animatronic humans (and animals) was a marvel to many guests, and its rollicking "Yo Ho, A Pirate's Life for Me" theme gave piracy a new and irresistibly party-like face.

18
March

DID YOU KNOW? ——————————————

Although for years the slightly befuddled voice of Sterling Holloway was identified with Pooh, Walt Disney initially approached comedian George Gobel about the job, but was turned down. (Since Holloway's death in 1992, the task has fallen primarily to voice specialist Jim Cummings, who took on the Pooh television series.)

19
March

(1959) *The Shaggy Dog,* the studios' first live-action comedy and an unexpectedly successful movie that grossed over $12 million, was released. The movie marked the first Disney appearance for Fred MacMurray, who would ultimately star in seven Disney films. MacMurray's supporting cast resembled a *Mickey Mouse Club* reunion: Annette Funicello, Tim Considine, and Tommy Kirk. The film had two sequels: the 1976 *Shaggy D.A.,* with Dean Jones as the grown-up Wilby; and *The Return of the Shaggy Dog,* a 1987 TV movie. A TV remake of the original film debuted in 1994, and a big-screen remake of *The Shaggy Dog,* starring Disney regular Tim Allen, was released in 2006.

BY THE NUMBERS ————————————

The Swiss Family Tree House at Walt Disney World in Orlando, called *Disneyodendron eximus* ("extraordinary Disney tree"), measures 90 feet across and 90 feet high, with roots nearly half as deep; it weighs more than 200 tons and has 1,400 branches and 300,000 individually attached plastic leaves.

(1991) A Los Angeles jury awarded singer Peggy Lee $3.8 million (eventually reduced to $2.3 million) in damages for her work in the 1955 *Lady and the Tramp*. Lee, who had cowritten six songs for the movie and provided voices for four characters, was originally paid $3,500. The movie was rereleased in 1962, 1971, 1980, and 1986 before being released on home video in 1987, a format that had not existed in 1955. Lee sued Disney for $50 million, claiming she had not authorized the use of her performances for the video versions, which grossed a reported $72 million.

20
March

DISNEY QUIZ

What scene from a Disney animated classic famously brought Walt Disney to tears every time he saw it?

In *Bambi*, the scene in which Bambi's mother is shot by hunters

LEGENDARY PEOPLE

Whose beautiful singing voice was personally chosen by Walt Disney in 1937 to help create one of the most famous animated leading ladies of all time?

Adriana Caselotti (aka Snow White), named a Disney Legend in 1994

21
March

(1975) *Escape to Witch Mountain,* which despite its name had more to do with science fiction than supernatural magic, was released. *Escape* tells the story of two orphans, 13-year-old Tony and his 11-year-old sister Tia, who have extraordinary psychic abilities and turn out to be castaways from another planet. The movie was so successful that a sequel, *Return from Witch Mountain,* was filmed and released in 1978, and the original was released on video three times before Disney remade it for television in 1995.

DID YOU KNOW?

Fred MacMurray, one of Disney's most popular movie stars, once told an interviewer that his roles in the non-Disney *Double Indemnity* and *The Apartment* represented "the only two parts I did in my entire career that required any acting."

DISNEY QUIZ

What is the meaning of the word Chakranadi, the name of the river in the Kali River Rapids ride at Walt Disney World's Animal Kingdom?

"Chakranadi" means "the river that runs in a circle"—as in fact this river does.

March

(1975) Lake Buena Vista Village, a shopping center at the edge of the Walt Disney World property, opened for business. Its name changed twice before it became Downtown Disney Marketplace in 1996, with the grand opening of the World of Disney superstore. At that time, it was combined with Pleasure Island and the West Side shopping area into a contiguous shopping, dining, and entertainment complex called Downtown Disney—a concept designed to encourage locals to patronize the Disney properties on a regular basis. Unlike most of Walt Disney World, the Marketplace requires no admission ticket.

NAME THAT 'TOON

At the 1937 Academy Awards ceremony, Walt Disney was invited to announce the Oscar for Best Cartoon Short Subject—and ended up presenting the statuette to himself. What cartoon won him the Oscar?

"The Country Cousin"

23

March

(1990) *Pretty Woman*, a hugely popular romantic comedy that became the studios' most successful live-action film to date and that made Julia Roberts into a full-fledged celebrity, was released. This modern-day *Pygmalion* became an immediate and unexpected hit. Still a newcomer, Julia Roberts was even nominated for an Academy Award for her performance as Vivian. The movie cost only about $14 million and grossed $463 million worldwide. It would remain the monetary standard until 1999, when *The Sixth Sense* earned $300 million in the United States alone.

DID YOU KNOW? ————————

The Winnie-the-Pooh franchise, with an estimated worth at around $6 billion a year, sparked a long and acrimonious court battle over royalty payments. A. A. Milne's will had divided the rights among several groups. The U.S. marketing rights were acquired by Stephen Slesinger, Inc., who then licensed them to Disney for $11 million a year. In the early 1990s, Slesinger accused Disney of not paying royalties on merchandise and video and DVD sales. In 2004, the case was dismissed with prejudice by a Los Angeles Superior Court judge.

(1901) Ub Iwerks, Walt Disney's first business partner and perhaps the greatest animator of all time, was born. Walt and Ub's first partnership, the Iwerks-Disney Studio, lasted a month before going bankrupt, but fortunately both men were hired by the Kansas City Slide Company. Two years later, when Walt set up Laugh-O-Gram Films, Ub came on board as chief animator. That venture didn't survive, but when Walt got the "Alice" comedies going and moved to California, Iwerks followed. Iwerks was quite important to Disney because, while Walt conceived of Mickey Mouse, Iwerks polished the mouse's profile. He animated "Steamboat Willie," the first Mickey Mouse cartoon released.

24
March

NAME THAT 'TOON

What holiday video collection contains five shorts titled "Belles on Ice," "Christmas: Impossible," "Donald's Gift," "Christmas Maximus," and "Mickey's Dog-Gone Christmas"?

Mickey's Twice upon a Christmas

25 March

(1996) Director John Lasseter, a former Disney animator, was honored with an Academy Award for special achievement for *Toy Story,* the first feature-length computer-animated film. By then, Lasseter was head of Pixar, Inc. But Lasseter's career began at Walt Disney Studios. In 1984, he took a month's leave from Disney to study at LucasFilm's Industrial Light & Magic; however, when Steve Jobs bought that studio six months later and renamed it Pixar, Lasseter went along. In the mid-1990s, by which time Pixar had a partnership with Disney, he wrote and directed the groundbreaking *Toy Story,* still one of the most successful films ever.

WHERE'S MICKEY?

In Dan Brown's thriller *The Da Vinci Code,* the hero, symbolist Robert Langdon, refuses to wear anything other than a vintage Mickey Mouse watch on his wrist.

(1911) Thornton Hee—whose pen name, T. Hee, was often assumed to be an inside joke—was born. A favorite caricaturist, Hee drew caricatures of Disney studios colleagues into the animated opening credits of *The Reluctant Dragon* and supplied the animated intro for the original *Parent Trap.* Hee also directed the "Dance of the Hours" segment of *Fantasia,* in which a troupe of hefty hippos in ballerina tutus perform with their slinky alligator partners; stilt-legged ostriches on toe enact dainty corps de ballet passages; and elephants try to disguise themselves behind pillars.

26
March

DISNEY QUIZ

What was the name of the ragtime and jazz band made up of Disney animators, writers, and technicians that recorded a dozen albums and headlined at Disneyland's Golden Horseshoe for many summers?

The Firehouse Five Plus Two. Ward Kimball served as Fire Chief and "designated trombonist."

27
March

(2004) One of the company's oldest "stars," Davy Crockett, was resurrected in a film called *The Alamo.* The movie's premiere in San Antonio, an old-fashioned celebrity spectacular, went weirdly awry when Jason Patric, who played faltering adventurer Jim Bowie, apparently drove to Austin after the premiere party to continue celebrating and was arrested on suspicion of public intoxication and allegedly resisting arrest. The story made national gossip columns, and it seems to have been an omen for this film, which got only a lukewarm reception when it was released on April 9.

BY THE NUMBERS

According to Christopher Finch in *The Art of Disney,* one scene in the 1937 Oscar-winning *The Old Mill*—the scene in which the camera zooms in on the village as the school bell rings and the pigeons soar and then settle along the roofs—cost $45,000, the equivalent of more than $300,000 today. The expense was due to the use of the new multiplane camera.

(2000) The ban was lifted on cast members' moustaches—which, considering Walt Disney's own, seems only fair. Disney has always maintained strict rules about the dress, hair, and even jewelry of "cast members" (the phrase applied to all Disney employees, up to and including the CEO). Sideburns must be a certain length. Beards, goatees, shaved heads, visible tattoos, excessive piercings—meaning anything other than in the earlobe, and only two holes there—are verboten. So are overly bright nail polish, extremely long nails, flashy jewelry, and bare legs; panty hose are required even with open-toed shoes.

NAME THAT 'TOON

What Disney-Pixar film boasted the talents, though only the narrative ones, of puppeteer icon and longtime Jim Henson collaborator Frank Oz as the voice of Fungus?

Monsters, Inc.

DISNEY QUIZ

For what were Snow White's dwarfs named when they were reintroduced in a two-hour movie from Hallmark Entertainment that aired on *The Wonderful World of Disney* in March 2002?

The seven days of the week

29
March

(1963) *Miracle of the White Stallions* premiered. Inspired by a true story, it portrays Viennese officer Col. Alois Podhajsky's efforts to save the horses of the Spanish Riding School in the last days of World War II. The Lippizaners, famous for their dance steps called "airs above the ground," were under threat in two arenas: the stallions were at the school in Vienna, which was being bombarded by German forces; but the mares in Czechoslovakia were directly in the path of the Soviet army. Podhajsky appealed to Gen. George S. Patton, and with the help of the U.S. Army, the stallions and mares were reunited and led to safety.

LEGENDARY PEOPLE ────────────

What longtime Disney animator and story man is thought to be the only person who worked on both *Fantasia* and *Fantasia/2000*?

Joe Grant, named a Disney Legend in 1992

(1968) On New York City's Lower East Side, two children found the body of a homeless man. The body was not claimed and was buried in Potter's Field; a year later, a finger-print match revealed that this was Bobby Driscoll, a longtime Disney star. At age 31, he had apparently died of a drug overdose. Driscoll's most famous roles included that of Johnny in *Song of the South,* Jeremiah Kincaid in *So Dear to My Heart,* and Jim Hawkins in *Treasure Island.* In 1949, the year he appeared in *So Dear to My Heart,* Driscoll was given a special juvenile Academy Award.

30
March

DISNEY QUIZ

Where does the title of the ABC game show *Who Wants to Be a Millionaire?,* which started in Britain in 1998, come from?

Cole Porter's 1956 hit song of the same name

DID YOU KNOW?

One concept drawing for the movie *Pinocchio* showed the *Mona Lisa* lying in a corner, possibly a comment on the artistic quality Walt Disney demanded of his animators.

31
March

(1999) The company announced it had bought all remaining shares of the Anaheim Angels baseball team from the estate of cowboy star Gene Autry for a reported $140 million. In November, Disney changed the team's name, added red halos to the "A" logo, and arranged a deal with Edison International to rename Anaheim Stadium "Edison Field." In 2002, the Angels won their first-ever World Series, defeating upstate rivals the San Francisco Giants. Even so, the team lost $10 million that year, and in 2003, Disney announced that the team would be sold to entrepreneur Arte Moreno for nearly $200 million.

DISNEY QUIZ

Who is the one U.S. president who never visited either Disneyland or Walt Disney World after their respective openings?

President Lyndon B. Johnson. (Yet he awarded Walt Disney the Medal of Freedom in 1964.)

April

A crowd of visitors walks to Sleeping Beauty's Castle at Disneyland Paris in Marne-La-Vallée, east of Paris, 1995.

1
April

(1995) Blizzard Beach, the third and largest of the aquatic parks in Walt Disney World, opened to the public. It covered 66 acres—eight times the size of River Country, Disney's first water adventure park—and featured 17 water slides, including the 120-foot-high and 360-foot-long Summit Plummet, down which riders may pick up speeds of as much as 60 mph. According to the legend, the park is the remains of a failed ski resort on the slopes of Mount Gushmore. Just as construction was complete, the weather supposedly reverted to normal levels and the resort went into physical as well as financial meltdown.

DISNEY QUIZ

What former Democratic president, as story has it, refused to ride Dumbo's Flying Elephants when he visited Disneyland, saying he couldn't possibly ride on the symbol of the Republican Party?

Harry Truman

April

(1940) The company—which until then had belonged only to Walt and Lilly Disney and Roy and Edna Disney—issued its first public stock offering: 155,000 shares of preferred stock at $25 a share, and 600,000 shares of common stock at $5 per share. The shares were snapped up, and the sale brought in $9 million, saving the day. Ironically, it also helped convince many employees that the studio was better off than it really was, which contributed to the unrest that finally led to the 1941 strike.

DID YOU KNOW?

Walt Disney World's version of Big Thunder Mountain was so realistic that when the Imagineers finished, a host of rattlesnakes tried to take up residence there.

BY THE NUMBERS

As the world's largest Disney character merchandise shop, the World of Disney megastore at Walt Disney World covers 50,000 square feet and racks up 10,000 sales every day.

3

April

(1994) Frank Wells, president of the Walt Disney Company and chairman Michael Eisner's closest working partner, was killed in a helicopter crash. He and Eisner, along with Jeffrey Katzenberg, who had come over with Eisner from Paramount to head up Disney's movie and television division, moved so quickly to restore Disney studios that within ten years, they had taken the company from $1.5 billion in revenue to $10 billion in revenue and an estimated net worth of five times that. Wells's death would bring on a bout of depression in Eisner, and eventually a series of corporate crises.

DID YOU KNOW?

The most popular attraction at Disney's California Adventure in Disneyland is Soarin' over California, a stunningly realistic hang-gliding ride on which "winged" chairs are hoisted 40 feet high and a 360-degree IMAX screen shows the Golden Gate Bridge, a grove of redwoods, and the cliffs of Yosemite, all while the "wind" whistles past and a spray of seawater splashes up from surfers.

(1956) The *Disneyland* show aired a segment called "Where Do the Stories Come From?" that featured Kirk Douglas and gave new and sometimes funny insights into the private lives of Walt Disney and his animators. The vignettes were often serious as well, since many of the gags and story lines in Donald Duck's wartime escapades were based on the real armed-services experiences of Walt and his staffers, some of whom had survived World War I.

4
April

LEGENDARY PEOPLE ───────────

What director of many Disney movies about horses was awarded the American Horse Show Association's Pegasus Medal of Honor in 2000 for his film work?

Larry Lansburgh, named a Disney Legend in 1998

5
April

(1965) *Mary Poppins* won five Academy Awards, including one for Julie Andrews as Best Actress. In her acceptance speech, she said, "Mr. Disney gets the biggest thanks." While *Mary Poppins* did not win Best Picture—that went to *My Fair Lady*—Andrews did beat out Audrey Hepburn in the actress category, a special win for her. Andrews had originated the role of Eliza Doolittle in *My Fair Lady* in London and eventually moved to Broadway. But for the movie version, Warner Bros. chose Hepburn for her star power. Hepburn may have worn the Cecil Beaton costumes well, but she couldn't sing. (That job fell to Marni Nixon, who also "voiced" Natalie Wood in *West Side Story*.)

NAME THAT 'TOON

What Academy Award-winning animated feature created by Japanese animator Hayao Miyazaki was partly backed by Disney, which distributed the film in the United States?

Spirited Away

6

April

(1971) Mickey Mouse appeared on the cover of *Look* magazine with a splashy headline calling him "the first citizen of Florida" and a story about Walt Disney World's creation.

(1978) Mickey was again the magazine's cover boy, but this time, celebrating his 50th birthday and fitting in with the cover story on the disco craze, Mickey appeared in a white outfit and in a pose parodying John Travolta's famous poster shot from *Saturday Night Fever*. The picture caused debate among the Disney faithful, but since it did not presage any permanent shift in Mickey's costume, most shrugged it off.

BY THE NUMBERS

While most animators can manage only 80 to 100 drawings a day, onetime Disney animator Ub Iwerks was a craftsman of extraordinary speed, famously turning out 700 drawings daily.

DISNEY QUIZ

What building in Marceline, Missouri, is named for Walt Disney, the town's most famous former resident?

The post office, named for Walt Disney in 2004 during its Disney celebration

7

April

(1939) "The Ugly Duckling," the 75th and last "Silly Symphony," was released. An earlier black-and-white rendition, released in 1931, portrays a mother hen who hatches a black duckling and then shoos him away in horror. When a tornado blows her chicks into a river, the duck saves them. He ends up not merely a member of the family but the favorite son. More faithful to the Hans Christian Andersen tale, the colorized remake depicts a mother swan finally recognizing a young "duckling" as one of her species and adopting him. The film won the Academy Award for Best Cartoon Short.

"I don't believe there's a challenge anywhere in the world that's more important to people everywhere than finding solutions to the problems of our great cities. [EPCOT] will always be in a state of becoming. It will never cease to be a living blueprint of the future."

—Walt Disney, in a 1966 videotape describing his vision of EPCOT Center, or what is now Epcot

(1974) The Treasure Island nature preserve opened at Walt Disney World. Treasure Island was little more than a scrub of beach and a hunting blind before Imagineers ordered up a few million pounds of exotic landscaping; 250 species of plants and trees from South and Central America and Asia; and 135 species of exotic birds and animals.

Treasure Island never attracted an audience, and in 1978 it was closed, renovated, and reopened as Discovery Island. The animals and plants became the main attraction, with a walk-through aviary, flamingo pond, and beach. In 1998, with the opening of Animal Kingdom, most of the wildlife from Discovery Island moved there and the island was closed.

8
April

DISNEY QUIZ

What soon-to-be talk show host provided the singing voice, though uncredited, of Prince Charming in Disney's 1950 *Cinderella*?

Mike Douglas, who also had a pop music hit in 1966 called "The Men in My Little Girl's Life"

9
April

(2005) Mickey Mouse led the 93rd-annual National Cherry Blossom Festival Parade in Washington, D.C., as grand marshal. He is believed to have been the first and only non-human to be grand marshal. The festival commemorates the Japanese government's gift to the United States of 3,000 flowering cherry trees, many of which are still visible around the Tidal Basin and Jefferson Memorial of the nation's capital. The two-week-long celebra-tion—which includes the lighting of a 350-year-old Japanese stone lantern, fireworks, a kite festival, and music and dance perfor-mances—marks the enduring friendship of the two nations.

DISNEY QUIZ

Upon what real geographical area was Disneyland's Big Thunder Mountain attraction based?

Bryce Canyon National Park in Utah

BY THE NUMBERS

The entire set of the Disney movie *The Alamo* (2004) spread across 51 acres in Texas, making it the largest freestanding set ever built in North America.

10
April

(2001) As part of a statewide observance of Walt Disney's 100th birthday, officials broke ground for an interactive museum on the site of Disney's Laugh-O-Gram studios in Kansas City, Missouri. Walt and his 11 employees used five rooms of the two-story brick building. In 1922, Disney borrowed $15,000 and convinced the owners of Newman's Theater to buy a series of cartoons instead of renting them from East Coast animators. The cartoons became known as Newman's Laugh-O-Grams. But Newman's declared bankruptcy six months later, and so did Disney. "If my grandfather were alive, he'd want to see this happen," said Walt Miller, Diane Disney Miller's son. "His career started in that building. I mean, there are fingerprints in that building of my grandfather."

NAME THAT 'TOON

What 1970s movie recycled bits of animation from earlier Disney films, including a bear doing Baloo's dance number from *The Jungle Book*, a singing cat reprising Scat Cat from *The Aristocats*, and a leading lady following the same dance sequence performed by Snow White?

Robin Hood

11

April

(1925) Roy O. Disney, Walt's brother, business partner, and most sincere admirer, married longtime girlfriend Edna Francis. It was a family affair: Elias and Flora Disney and Herbert Disney came to the wedding, which was held at Uncle Robert Disney's home. Walt was his brother's best man, and Walt's girlfriend, Lillian Bounds, an "ink-and-paint girl" that Walt had begun dating, served as Edna's maid of honor. After Walt married Lilly only three months later, the four were nearly always together. In 1927, the Disney brothers purchased adjoining lots and built identical houses.

DISNEY QUIZ

Which Disney executive was born on the Disneyland property—back when it was an orange grove?

Ron Dominguez. His family was one of the 17 that sold their land to Walt Disney in 1954. He figures that his family's lot is under what is now the Rivers of America.

(1992) Euro Disneyland and the Euro Disney resort, a joint venture with the French government, opened outside Paris. The press condemned it as a "cultural Chernobyl," and the French voiced widespread concern about the possible "Americanization" of their country. Only 6,000 people came on opening day.

Ambivalent or not, the French couldn't stay away entirely. By the park's first anniversary, more than 10 million guests had passed through the gates, and 100 million by January 2001. The park's name was changed to Disneyland Paris in October 1994.

12
April

DID YOU KNOW?

Famed conductor Arturo Toscanini called the 1935 Mickey Mouse cartoon "The Band Concert" his personal favorite and reportedly saw it six times.

13
April

(1965) Walt and Roy Disney and other Disney staffers traveled to Huntsville, Alabama, at the invitation of Dr. Wernher von Braun, to tour the George C. Marshall Space Flight Center. Braun apparently hoped Disney would film a television show or even a movie about the space program, and for a while it seemed likely. Disney declared that if he could use his TV show "to wake people up to the fact that we've got to keep exploring, I'll do it." The next morning's headline on the *Huntsville Times* read, curiously, "Disney Makes Pledge to Aid Space." However, no further collaboration ever occurred, and Walt died the next year.

WHERE'S MICKEY?

In 2003, as part of Mickey's 75th-birthday celebration, 75 of the mouse's celebrity friends designed six-foot statues expressing their personal sense of Mickey's importance. The 75 statues went on tour, spending six weeks at Washington's Ronald Reagan International Trade Center. At the end of the tour, Sotheby's auctioned them off and donated all proceeds to charity. Among the celebrities who created custom Mickeys were basketball star Shaquille O'Neal; tennis icon Andre Agassi; Mouseketeer superstar Annette Funicello; daytime-drama queen Susan Lucci; and actors John Travolta, Jennifer Garner, and Ben Affleck.

14
April

(2000) The Orlando Rays, the AA affiliate of the Tampa Bay Devil Rays, opened their first season at home at Cracker Jack Stadium in the Wide World of Sports at Walt Disney World. They won 70 games in the Southern League before the season ended August 31. Although the team played in the state-of-the-art stadium that the Atlanta Braves used for spring training—and although they won three Southern League championships while in Orlando—attendance for the Rays' games was not good. After four seasons at Disney World, and after 30 years in Orlando, the team was moved to Montgomery, Alabama, and renamed the Biscuits.

DISNEY QUIZ

In the 1946 Goofy cartoon "Double Dribble," what group of people's real names are found on the backs of the basketball teams' jerseys?

Disney artists

BY THE NUMBERS

Imagineers estimated that the audio-animatronic Abe Lincoln that performed at the 1964–65 New York World's Fair was capable of more than 250,000 combinations of physical action.

15
April

(1983) Tokyo Disneyland, the first Disney property built outside the United States, opened in Urayasu, Japan, just outside Tokyo. It instantly became the world's most visited amusement park. It has drawn more than 10 million visitors every year since it opened and, in the 1996–97 fiscal year, set a record with 17.4 million guests.

On September 4, 2001, a second theme park opened in the area: Tokyo DisneySea, a 100-acre aquatic park with seven "ports of call" featuring restaurants, attractions, and shops. A stunning success, DisneySea lured its 10 millionth guest in less than a year of its opening.

DID YOU KNOW?

According to Imagineer Rolly Crump, while he and Yale Gracey were working on the Haunted Mansion ride, their workroom was so littered with skeletons and eerie paraphernalia that the cleaning crew asked that the lights be kept on at night. Instead, Gracey and Crump rigged the lights so that when the switch was flipped, the skeletons would leap up. The janitors fled and never returned to work.

(2001) Situated alongside the Animal Kingdom, the spectacular Animal Kingdom Lodge at Walt Disney World opened to the public. With three savannah areas over 33 acres providing views of gazelles, giraffes, zebras, and more, it's the closest thing to a safari Imagineers could provide. The re-created African landscape influenced the hotel's design as well. The lobby is a four-story atrium crossed by a hanging bridge, lit by chandeliers that resemble tribal shields or exotic flowers, and stocked with African sculptures. In addition to 1,300 rooms and two spas, the hotel also has an 11,000-square-foot swimming pool with a 67-foot slide.

16
April

DISNEY QUIZ

What father and son team appeared in both *The Absent-Minded Professor* and *Son of Flubber?*

Ed Wynn and Keenan Wynn

LEGENDARY PEOPLE

What acting father and daughter can both be found on the Disney Legend list, with the daughter receiving the nod before her dad?

John Mills, named a Disney Legend in 2002, and Hayley Mills, named a Disney Legend in 1998

17
April

(1961) *The Horse with the Flying Tail* received an Academy Award for Best Documentary Feature of 1960. An equine Cinderella story, the film recounts the true tale of a talented but mistreated palomino cow horse who was rescued by Bertalan de Nemethy, then coach of the United States Equestrian Team. Given a new name, Nautical, and partnered with former Navy man Hugh Wiley as his rider, the pair won the team gold medal at the 1959 Pan Am Games and took prizes in the 1958 and 1959 European Games. In 1959, Nautical and Wiley won the King George V cup, the most valuable sporting trophy in the world.

DISNEY QUIZ

What Disney cartoon character's heartthrob was Dinah the dachshund, who appeared in five features with him?

Pluto

NAME THAT 'TOON

What film did animator Ollie Johnston say was 40 years in the making, with the idea beginning "probably before *Cinderella*"?

Beauty and the Beast

(1994) The live musical version of *Beauty and the Beast* debuted at the Palace Theater in Times Square, after previews in Houston, Texas. The next day, the show set a Broadway record by selling $700,000 in tickets. *Beauty* would become one of Broadway's longest-running hits, and it was one of three Disney musicals in production on Broadway—along with *The Lion King* and *Aida*—at the same time. *Beauty* was nominated for nine Tony Awards but won only one, for costume designer Ann Hould-Ward, who had the difficult task of making the candlesticks and cutlery not only three-dimensional but also flexible enough for dancing.

18
April

DID YOU KNOW?

Russi Taylor, the voice of Minnie Mouse since 1986, has also voiced such characters as Donald's nephews Huey, Louie, and Dewey; Muppet Baby Gonzo; and Pebbles Flintstone.

19
April

(1955) Jackson Gillis was paid $500 for an outline of a screenplay based on a book by Lawrence Edward Watkin called *Marty Markham,* about a bunch of boys at the Triple R dude ranch. Under its new name, *The Adventures of Spin and Marty,* the show launched one of *The Mickey Mouse Club's* most popular segments, a serial that ran for three seasons and nearly 200 episodes. Actor Tim Considine, who read for both roles during casting, persuaded *Club* producer Bill Walsh that he was better suited for Spin than the pampered Marty, and Spin's role was beefed up to make the two boys costars.

DISNEY QUIZ

According to publicity flyers, what was the recipe for Flubber, the antigravity-prone goo introduced in the 1961 movie *The Absent-Minded Professor?*

Combine saltwater taffy, a dash of polyurethane foam, baker's yeast, cracked rice, and molasses. Boil until it lifts lid and says, "Qurp." (Or fans could more safely buy the Hasbro version.)

April

(1946) *Make Mine Music,* a sort of pop-music sequel to *Fantasia* featuring ten cartoon shorts set to the music of Benny Goodman, Dinah Shore, and the Andrews Sisters—and introducing Sergei Prokofiev's *Peter and the Wolf* to the world—had its New York premiere. It would go into general release in August. One of the best segments, "The Whale Who Wanted to Sing at the Met" features Nelson Eddy as a whale who dreams he is making his operatic debut. But in the real, waking world, he has been harpooned because he's believed to have swallowed the real singer.

"To know [Walt Disney] was to know that we had been fortunate to have a spirit with us that perhaps comes once in a generation. He was a great artist. He was a perfectionist. He was a wonderful human being. . . . The world is a better and a happier and a more joyful place in which to live because he was there."

—Richard Nixon, at the opening of EPCOT in 1982

21
April

(2005) One of the crowning achievements of Disney Imagineering, the first peripatetic and apparently "intelligent" audio-animatronic creation, made its debut at the Animal Kingdom at Walt Disney World. Lucky the Dinosaur is his own freestanding attraction, and the first in a revolutionary generation of such creatures. Lucky walks upright on large back legs, balances a long tail, and is derived from the *Tyrannosaurus rex* silhouette but softened. Approximately 9 feet tall and 12 feet long, Lucky drags a flower cart and signs autographs by drawing a flower. He spent most of the summer at Animal Kingdom before leaving to participate in the opening of Hong Kong Disneyland.

BY THE NUMBERS —————————————

The largest production ever filmed at London's Pinewood studios, the six-hour *Wonderful World of Disney* miniseries called *Dinotopia* (2002) required the construction of 42 sets, and the Waterfall City set alone covered five acres and cost $50,000 a day just to keep up. The computer animation was so complex that an average of 28 minutes of film was produced each day, resulting in about 1 minute of usable footage.

April

(1964) The New York World's Fair in Queens, where Walt Disney tried out several of what were to become his parks' most popular attractions, opened. Disney contributed four attractions to the World's Fair, all of which incorporated audio-animatronic figures. They included a model-scale Disneyland that became It's a Small World; the original Carousel of Progress, then called "Progressland," in the General Electric Pavilion; the Ford Rotunda, which held the Magic Skyway, later moved to Disneyland; and the Illinois Pavilion where, on May 2, "Great Moments with Mr. Lincoln" would premiere.

DISNEY QUIZ

What Disney family member claimed he was the model for the lovable Goofy?

Roy E. Disney

April

(1923) Walt Disney signed a contract with his first star, a six-year-old Kansas City actress named Virginia Davis, to appear in a short Laugh-O-Gram film called *Alice's Wonderland*. Never actually released, this short film got Walt his first contract with distributor Margaret Winkler. Virginia Davis was so important to the project, Walt thought, that he persuaded her parents to move to California when he and Roy did, so she could continue to play the part. Eventually, 56 "Alice" comedies were released, and over the years three other girls, Margie Gay, Dawn O'Day, and Lois Hardwick, starred as Alice.

DISNEY QUIZ

What is the real name of Hungarian writer Felix Salten, who wrote the novel on which *Bambi* is based?

Seigmund Salzmann

NAME THAT 'TOON

What movie's Oscar-winning title song was recorded twice: once by Angela Lansbury for the film itself, and then by Celine Dion and Peabo Bryson for the final credits?

Beauty and the Beast (1991)

24

April

(1989) The Disney Channel aired the first episode of a third-generation *Mickey Mouse Club,* launching a handful of performers to popularity heights scarcely dreamed of by their predecessors. One cast member, Britney Spears, eclipsed even Annette Funicello as the biggest little Mouseketeer of them all. (Other famous former players include Justin Timberlake, Christina Aguilera, and J. C. Chasez of 'NSync.) This third series was referred to as *MMC,* in an attempt to shake off the goody-two-shoes image of the previous two clubs and to draw in the MTV generation; and the cast members were never referred to as Mouseketeers. The show ran for a little more than five years.

DID YOU KNOW?

During the recording sessions for the 1988 TV special "Totally Minnie," Minnie Mouse's voice, Russi Taylor, met Mickey Mouse's voice, Wayne Allwine, and they fell in love and married.

April

(1929) "The Barnyard Battle," the first cartoon to place Mickey in a combat situation, was released. Directed by Walt Disney, it features Mickey's rival Pete in the company of a cat army that invades the mice homeland. Mickey eventually forces the cats to retreat and becomes a hero to his look-alike compatriots. Although it has light moments, "Barnyard Battle" exhibits a darker side. In the cartoon's most famous sequence, Mickey undergoes a somewhat rough and emotionally abusive physical examination before being handed a machine gun and packed off to the "front."

DID YOU KNOW? ————————————————

In the beginning, the narrator of the Goofy "How To" cartoons, animator John McLeish, was not told that the script was a joke and that Goofy would be doing everything backward. The deadpan narration that resulted is partly responsible for the series' success.

April

(2005) Panicked bride-to-be Jennifer Wilbanks fled her approaching nuptials in Duluth, Georgia, and became, like the title of a successful Disney film, America's "runaway bride." Disney's *Runaway Bride* movie, released in the summer of 1999, tried to cash in on the huge success of *Pretty Woman,* reuniting Julia Roberts, Richard Gere, Hector Elizondo, and director Garry Marshall. The film was popular enough that when a real-life bride-to-be made headlines, people instantly applied the movie title to her. Wilbanks's escapade inspired a runaway-bride action figure, which Julia Roberts had not.

DISNEY QUIZ

What Disney animated character was chosen by the French Olympic team in 1980 as their mascot?

Goofy, who had starred in a series of "How To" sports shorts

NAME THAT 'TOON

What was the last Disney film to employ CAPS (Computer Animation Production System) technology?

Home on the Range (2004)

April

(2003) *The Wonderful World of Disney* aired a version of *Eloise at the Plaza,* based on Kay Thompson's children's books about the spoiled, impulsive, but good-hearted six-year-old who lives at New York's Plaza Hotel with her nanny, her pets, and occasionally her flighty socialite mother. It starred Disney's most famous governess, Julie Andrews, as Eloise's nanny, and coming only two years after her starring role in the Disney film *The Princess Diaries* it suggested a comfortable return home by the former Mary Poppins.

LEGENDARY PEOPLE ————————————

What Disney voice-over artist's non-Disney credits include singing "You're a Mean One, Mister Grinch" in the 1966 Chuck Jones classic version of *How the Grinch Stole Christmas*?

Thurl Ravenscroft, named a Disney Legend in 1995

(1989) Pleasure Island, Walt Disney World's after-dark entertainment area, opened for cast members to preview. It officially opened to the public on May 1. This adult-nightlife area was designed to draw Orlando residents away from the downtown club district called Church Street Station. But it would also help the Disney Company maintain older visitors' allegiance and cater to young adults who wanted to continue partying after their children tired. Guests buy one ticket to gain admission to all clubs, which don't open until after 7 p.m., and they get a plastic bracelet that indicates they're over 21 and free to drink.

28
April

DISNEY QUIZ

What were some of the names by which Goofy was known before the moniker "Goofy" firmly stuck?

Dippy Dawg (in early newspaper cartoons), Dippy the Goof (in a 1938 book), and Mr. Geef (for a time in the 1950s)

29
April

(1957) Sleeping Beauty Castle opened in the Fantasyland area of Disneyland at Anaheim. Sleeping Beauty Castle was designed by Herb Ryman, the visionary who, over one weekend in 1953, drew nearly the entire plan for Disneyland to show New York TV executives. A tree alongside the castle is Ryman's memorial. Like most of the theme park structures, the castle employs forced perspective—in this case, diminishing-size "stones"—to make the building seem larger. However, Walt did not want the structure to be overwhelming, so he kept it relatively small, only 77 feet above moat level.

DISNEY QUIZ

What celebrated author brought the story of Bambi, from a novel written by Felix Salten, to Walt Disney's attention?

Thomas Mann

BY THE NUMBERS

Disney's *Pearl Harbor* (2001) had the largest preapproved film budget in Hollywood history, at $135 million with an additional $5 million of wiggle room.

30

April

(1989) The grand opening of Disney-MGM Studios at Walt Disney World was broadcast on TV as a preview to the official public opening May 1. Among the celebrity cameos was an appearance by Ronald Reagan, who had helped host the televised opening of Disneyland 34 years before. The show, which featured such Hollywood icons as George Burns, Estelle Getty, Tony Randall, Mickey Rooney, and Jimmy Stewart, as well as many younger stars, concluded with a spectacular "Hooray for Hollywood" production number that won choreographer Walter Painter an Emmy Award.

DID YOU KNOW?

Credit for the "I'm going to Disney World!" promotion campaign should go to Michael Eisner's wife, Jane. The first of the "I'm going to Disney World!" commercials aired on January 25, 1987, at the end of Super Bowl XXI, when New York Giants quarterback Phil Simms said the now famous words. Over the next 17 years, the Disney Company capitalized on the Olympics, the World Series, the NBA championships, even the Miss America contest. Most of the commercials were filmed twice: once for the Anaheim Disneyland and once for Orlando's Disney World (or four times, in some cases, since the outcome of certain sports events was unknown). In January 2005, Disney officials announced that they would discontinue the campaign, and Super Bowl MVP Tom Brady had to make his own vacation plans.

May

Mickey and Minnie Mouse, Pluto, and trumpeters help mark the opening of the Disney Store on New York's Fifth Avenue, 1996.

(1989) Pleasure Island, the first Disney park aimed almost exclusively at an adult audience, opened at Walt Disney World in Orlando. With a single admission price, guests can dance at the BET Soundstage, participate in a half-improv comedy contest at the Comedy Warehouse, or travel back in time at the Adventurers Club, a pre–World War II British explorers' club and music hall that's nearly an amusement park by itself. The middle of the island has an outdoor stage where each evening ends with a "New Year's Eve" party.

1

May

DID YOU KNOW? ————

Presidential visits to Disney theme parks are a tradition: former President Harry Truman visited Disneyland in 1957. Former President Dwight D. Eisenhower went to Disneyland in 1961, the same year then-President John F. Kennedy visited. Richard Nixon made several trips to Disneyland beginning shortly after its opening in 1955 and was at Disney World for the opening of Epcot in 1982. Former President Gerald Ford went to Walt Disney World in 1979. Jimmy Carter went to Disneyland in 1978 and was photographed jogging past "America Sings." George H. W. Bush first visited Walt Disney World as vice president in 1983 and returned as president in 1990 and 1991. President Bill Clinton visited Disney World in 1996; and George W. Bush went there in 2003.

May

(1964) After weeks of delay, "Great Moments with Mr. Lincoln" opened at the New York World's Fair in Flushing Meadows, Queens, marking a watershed moment in entertainment. Before an audience of 500 at a time, the first great audio-animatronic character, an eerily precise re-creation of Walt Disney's favorite president, stood up from his chair and moved his hands and eyes as he spoke. Lincoln's address was a compilation of several of his memorable remarks covering freedom and civil rights. His voice was originally provided by Royal Dano, a veteran Abe impersonator who resembled Lincoln physically and had portrayed him in films.

NAME THAT 'TOON

What cartoon, inspired by a song by Oliver Wallace, shows Donald Duck making Chip and Dale "pedal" the bicycle he's riding to Daisy's house by running in the wheels like hamsters?

"Crazy over Daisy" (1950)

DISNEY QUIZ

What creature lurks in a dungeon underneath the castle at Disneyland Paris?

A sleeping audio-animatronic dragon that awakes in the company of park guests

(1969) Ground was broken for the Valencia campus of the California Institute of the Arts, generally known as CalArts, which was created by a merger of the Chouinard Art Institute and the Los Angeles Conservatory of Music. Construction of the 60-acre site was largely made possible by a bequest in Walt Disney's will. Veteran Disney animators taught and served as advisers at the school, and many of the students moved from there into Disney apprenticeships. CalArts helped revitalize Disney's art departments by supplying not only animators but special effects and background and layout artists.

3

May

DISNEY QUIZ

The name Bambi is short for what Italian word?

Bambino ("child")

NAME THAT 'TOON

In what 1929 cartoon was Mickey Mouse's speaking voice first heard?

"Karnival Kid"

4 May

(1949) *Seal Island*, the first "True-Life Adventure" featurette, went into general release. It won an Academy Award for Best Documentary, but it also represented a moral victory for Walt Disney, who had launched the film himself because RKO executives did not believe moviegoers would sit still for a half-hour nature film. Edited out of footage from Alaska shot by husband and wife cinematographers Alfred and Elma Milotte, the film shows the life cycle of seals, which return each year to the Pribilof Islands to mate and pup. Eventually Disney would release another dozen "True-Life Adventures" and win seven more Academy Awards.

DID YOU KNOW?

On July 19, 2002, the Disney Company announced it would probably build China's second theme park in Shanghai, but CEO-designate Robert Iger said later he did not expect that to happen before 2010—a change that in part reflected company concerns over pirating of movies in China and the government's reluctance to enforce copyright laws.

5

May

(2005) The official 18-month celebration of Disneyland's 50th birthday was launched at Walt Disney World in Orlando. Called "The Happiest Celebration on Earth," the birthday party was used as a promotional campaign to draw attention to Disney parks everywhere. As part of the campaign, each of Disney World's four parks featured attractions from the Disney parks in California, Paris, and Tokyo, while new attractions—and the 11th Disney theme park, Hong Kong Disneyland—opened around the globe. The celebration was presaged by a television commercial featuring such Disney characters as Dumbo, Goofy, and the Love Bug all "coming home" for the party.

LEGENDARY PEOPLE

Who wrote a song recorded by everyone from Tennessee Ernie Ford and Steve Allen to Mitch Miller, Burl Ives, the Sons of the Pioneers, and *Your Show of Shows* (and later *Days of Our Lives*) star Bill Hayes?

"The Ballad of Davy Crockett" composer George Bruns, named a Disney Legend in 2001

6
May

(1987) Lillian Bounds Disney, Walt's widow, announced the formation of a fund to construct the Walt Disney Concert Hall in Los Angeles, and she kicked it off with a donation of $50 million. The hall was intended to be a new home for the Los Angeles Philharmonic Orchestra, along with a performance space called the Roy and Edna Disney/CalArts Theater, or REDCAT. Frank Gehry was chosen as chief architect in 1991, and ground was broken in 1992. Unfortunately, due to years of mostly financial delays, Lillian would not live to see the building completed. The formal ribbon cutting took place on October 29, 2003.

DISNEY QUIZ

At what Walt Disney World venue will you find shrunken heads, a haunted library with a "ghost"-playing piano, and a secret handshake?

The Adventurers Club on Pleasure Island

DID YOU KNOW?

Richard Nixon delivered his famous "I am not a crook" speech at Walt Disney World in 1974.

May

(2001) The Walt Disney Company formally applied for approval from the Anaheim, California, Planning Commission to add a third park to the Disneyland and Disney's California Adventure complex. Although details were not announced, earlier reports had suggested it might either be a water park based on Typhoon Lagoon at Walt Disney World or an amusement park based on the Tokyo DisneySeas concept. The new park, originally scheduled to open in 2010 (though the opening is since rumored to be pushed back), will cover 78 acres and serve to join the 55-acre Disneyland with the 75-acre California Adventure.

"Walt Disney's greatest gifts to mankind were laughter, his steadfast faith in future generations, and his belief that good will ultimately triumph over evil."

— 1968 joint resolution of the Congress of the United States and the House of Representatives posthumously awarding Walt Disney the Congressional Gold Medal

8
May

(1893) Francis Ouimet, one of golf's real-life Cinderella stories, was born in Brookline, Massachusetts. More than a century later, the story of his stunning upset over English champions Harry Vardon and Ted Ray in the 1913 U.S. Open inspired the film *The Greatest Game Ever Played,* which starred Disney Channel favorite Shia LaBeouf and premiered in September 2005.

The first amateur ever to win the Open, Ouimet's victory became front-page news and was the first step toward the wider popularization of golf. The great golf writer Herbert Warren Wind called him "America's idea of the American hero."

BY THE NUMBERS ————————————————

By 1994, just eight years after "Disney's World on Ice" first traveled outside the United States, there were seven skating troupes performing simultaneously on six continents.

9
May

(1954) Walt and Lillian Disney's daughter Diane married a Stanford football player named Ronald W. Miller. Early on, Walt told Herb Ryman, "I have a great ambition for him. He will run the studio one day." In 1957, Walt hired him as a liaison between WED, the Imagineering division, and the construction crews at Disneyland; then as an assistant director of TV and movie projects; and eventually as a producer. Miller became executive producer of movies and TV in 1968 and served as president of Walt Disney Productions from 1980 to 1984, when he was defeated by Roy Disney's campaign to bring in Michael Eisner.

DISNEY QUIZ

At the Adventurers Club on Pleasure Island at Walt Disney World, what is the "secret" password?

"Kungaloosh!"

10
May

(1956) Paige O'Hara, the voice of Belle in *Beauty and the Beast* and its several sequels, and later Fantine in the Broadway production of *Les Misérables,* was born in Fort Lauderdale.

(1959) Walt and Lilly Disney's younger daughter, Sharon, married architect Robert Brown in a Pacific Palisades church. The date Sharon chose proved how close she was to her older sister: Diane had married Ron Miller on May 9, 1954, so now they could celebrate their anniversaries together.

NAME THAT 'TOON

What was the first cartoon in which Mickey Mouse wore his trademark white gloves, which he hasn't taken off in more than 75 years?

"The Opry House" (1929)

DISNEY QUIZ

Besides *Bambi,* what two other Disney hits did Felix Salten's writing inspire?

Perri, a Disney "True-Life Fantasy"; and *The Shaggy Dog,* based on the story *The Hound of Florence*

11

May

(1904) Surrealist painter Salvador Dalí was born in Figueras, Catalonia. Although the mild Walt Disney and the flamboyant Dalí may seem unlikely partners, they were great admirers of one another's creations. At a dinner party in 1946, Disney mentioned his interest in a cartoon based on a Spanish-language ballad by Armando Domínguez called "Destino." Dalí, then working with Alfred Hitchcock on *Spellbound,* was intrigued. For about eight months Dalí worked on the project, which was eventually abandoned. He died in 1989. Decades later, using computer animation and computer-generated imagery, "Destino" was completed. It premiered at the Annecy International Animation Festival in June 2003.

WHERE'S MICKEY?

At the Big Thunder Ranch, a re-creation of an 1880s working ranch that was paired with the Disneyland attraction Big Thunder Mountain from 1986 to 1996, visitors could see the famous Mickey Moo, a heifer born with a three-circle spot shaped like Mickey Mouse's head on her flank.

12
May

(2002) *Dinotopia,* a six-hour, $86 million miniseries from Hallmark Entertainment, premiered on *The Wonderful World of Disney.* A hugely complex combination of live action and digital computer animation, it was broadcast on three consecutive nights and inspired a follow-up series on ABC that ran for five weeks around the end-of-the-year holidays. Based on the popular illustrated books by James Gurney, the miniseries told of an alternate universe in which dinosaurs, or at least some species, and humans have coexisted in a near-utopian society for centuries.

DID YOU KNOW?

It has been widely reported that Michael Eisner had never actually seen a Disney movie until taking over the company.

DISNEY QUIZ

According to the strict employee dress policy at Disney theme parks, how large may female cast members' earrings be?

No larger than a quarter. (This rule has actually been relaxed over the years; women's earrings were originally limited to studs, then to nothing larger than a nickel.)

13
May

(2001) *Child Star,* a biopic of Shirley Temple based on her 1988 autobiography, aired on *The Wonderful World of Disney.* Surprisingly, this was the first time she had appeared in a Disney film, even being portrayed by someone else. (That "someone" was Emily Ann Hart, sister to Melissa Joan Hart, star of *Sabrina the Teenage Witch.*)

Despite never acting for Disney, Temple had several Disney connections: she presented Walt with the special Academy Award for *Snow White and the Seven Dwarfs* in 1939, she dedicated Sleeping Beauty Castle at Disneyland in 1957, and she served on Disney's board of directors from 1974 to 1975.

BY THE NUMBERS

Walt Disney World is the largest consumer of fireworks in North America, producing more than 11,000 shows per year and exploding more than one million projectiles and displays, each one hand-wrapped.

14

May

(1944) *Star Wars* creator George Lucas, whose films have inspired several of Disney's most popular attractions, was born in Modesto, California. The first collaboration between LucasFilms and Disney was the 17-minute, $17 million "Captain Eo," a music-video vehicle for then-megastar Michael Jackson that ran from 1986 until 1994 at Epcot and until 1997 at Disneyland. In 1987, Star Tours was unveiled at Disneyland in Anaheim, followed by versions at Disney-MGM Studios in Orlando, Tokyo Disneyland, and Disneyland Paris. The Orlando venue has become the home site of an annual series of *Star Wars* weekends that attract thousands every year.

DID YOU KNOW?

According to an urban legend, at the ceremony where he received the Presidential Medal of Freedom, the staunchly Republican Walt Disney flaunted his political loyalties and implicitly insulted President Lyndon Johnson by wearing a Barry Goldwater for President pin on his lapel.

15
May

(1856) L. Frank Baum, who created the wonderland known as Oz, was born. The most famous film version of his stories, *The Wizard of Oz,* was not made by Walt Disney, of course, but an Oz series had long been a project of Disney's. In 1954, Disney purchased the rights to 11 of the Oz books from Baum's son Robert, with the plan to make a special for the *Disneyland* show. But with the Judy Garland movie becoming a national TV tradition, Walt Disney got nervous and abandoned the project. Disney finally released an Oz feature—the part–live action, part-puppet "Return to Oz"—in 1985, nearly 30 years later than planned.

NAME THAT 'TOON

What was the Disney Company's first truly musical cartoon, in the sense that it used original music?

"The Opry House" (1929)

DISNEY QUIZ

At the 2005 Nights of Joy contemporary Christian music festival at Disney World, attendees were given advance copies of the soundtrack to what film?

The Lion, the Witch and the Wardrobe

16

May

(1916) Adriana Caselotti, who gave voice to the heroine of *Snow White and the Seven Dwarfs,* was born in Bridgeport, Connecticut. Caselotti, whose delicate and clear soprano is far more familiar than her name or face, was only 18 years old when she beat out 150 other girls for the role of Snow White. Some Disney staffers thought the role required a stronger voice, but the childlike quality of Caselotti's voice appealed to Walt Disney because it emphasized the character's innocence. After the release of *Snow White,* Caselotti appeared in small film roles and made radio appearances as a singer and voice actor.

"I have come to Hollywood and am in touch with the three great American surrealists—the Marx Brothers, Cecil B. DeMille, and Walt Disney."

—*Painter Salvador Dalí, writing to surrealist theorist André Breton in 1937*

DISNEY QUIZ

When forming their first partnership in 1920, why did Walt Disney and Ub Iwerks decide to call their studio Iwerks-Disney, rather than the other way around?

They were afraid the name Disney-Iwerks would sound like an eyewear manufacturer.

May

(1908) Joe Grant, who worked for Disney for more than 70 years, was born in New York. He created the character model department, which worked out stories and characters for the films and made three-dimensional models for the characters. Grant was first hired during the creation of "Mickey's Gala Premiere." Over the years, he headed up story development for *Fantasia,* worked on character development for *Pinocchio,* cowrote *Dumbo,* conceived of *Lady and the Tramp,* and designed Mrs. Potts for *Beauty and the Beast.* He was named a Disney Legend in 1992. Grant suffered a fatal heart attack at his drawing table days short of his 97th birthday.

DID YOU KNOW?

Before becoming Disney's second-longest-running CEO, Michael Eisner was vice president of ABC Entertainment, where he added *All My Children* and *One Life to Live* to the ABC afternoon lineup and worked on the long-running *General Hospital.* He also invented *Happy Days* while waiting out a snowstorm in the Newark airport and approved *Welcome Back, Kotter,* which launched the career of John Travolta.

18

May

(1911) Larry Lansburgh, who directed many of Disney's films about horses, was born in San Francisco. Earlier in his career, Lansburgh worked on such animated features as *Fantasia* and *Cinderella*. But for 30 years, Lansburgh specialized in films on animals; his first Oscar nomination was for *Cow Dog* in 1956, and his first Oscar came the next year, for *Wetback Hound*. But he had an affinity for horses, often making them into misunderstood heroes who are rescued after enduring danger or disappointment. His most famous film, and an Academy Award winner, is *The Horse with the Flying Tail*.

DISNEY QUIZ

What is Mickey Mouse called in China?

Mi Laoshu

(1960) *Pollyanna,* one of Disney's most popular live-action children's films, was released. It marked the Disney debut of 12-year-old Hayley Mills, who was to become one of the studios' most valued stars, and who won an Oscar for outstanding juvenile performance of the year. Yet the film was not the success Walt had expected, which he later decided was because the title made it sound too much like a "girl movie." Filming the story of the eternally optimistic orphan who comes to live with her wealthy aunt (played by Jane Wyman) cost $2.5 million.

19
May

NAME THAT 'TOON

What was the last film to depend primarily on hand-painted cels and the first to use, though in very limited footage, the CAPS technology, which allows handmade animation drawings to be copied and colored electronically?

The Little Mermaid (1989)

May

(1997) The lavishly restored New Amsterdam Theater in New York reopened with the world concert premiere of *Alan Menken and Tim Rice's King David*. Since November 1997, the theater has showcased the Tony Award–winning musical *The Lion King*. Once home to the Ziegfeld Follies and one of New York's premiere venues, the original Amsterdam had fallen into disrepair. Starting in 1995, Disney Imagineers restored much of it, including the ornate reliefs of gargoyles and the allegorical murals. The $40 million renovation was part of a campaign to return Times Square and 42nd Street to its former glory, and make a home for the Disney Company's growing live-entertainment industry.

BY THE NUMBERS

As of 2004, the median income for a family living in Celebration, Florida, the planned community built by the Disney Company, was $92,000.

May

(2001) Four days before the film's general release, the expensive *Pearl Harbor* was screened at a $5 million premiere aboard the nuclear aircraft carrier U.S.S. *John C. Stennis* stationed at Pearl Harbor, Hawaii. Some 2,000 military officials, veterans, and celebrities watched as survivors of the attack walked the red carpet, Navy SEALS jumped from a Black Hawk helicopter, and Hawaiian Air National Guard F-15 pilots flew overhead—all within yards of the U.S.S. *Arizona* wreckage beneath the water. The movie bombed domestically, grossing less than $200 million in the United States, but it managed to gross $450 million worldwide.

DISNEY QUIZ

In the Disney blockbuster *Pretty Woman,* what opera do Edward and his "date," Vivian, attend together?

Verdi's *La Traviata* ("The Fallen Woman"), also about a prostitute with a heart of gold

May

(1987) *Ernest Goes to Camp,* the first feature film starring Jim Varney as the well-meaning, hapless, but eternally optimistic Ernest P. Worrell, was released. The film, its six sequels, and a TV offshoot made the rubber-faced and elastic-voiced Varney a celebrity. Surprisingly, Varney was a classically trained actor, and he found it both amusing and frustrating to have made his reputation as Everyman Ernest, a character he had invented for a series of milk commercials. Varney died of a brain tumor in 2000.

LEGENDARY PEOPLE

Who was the voice of Donald Duck for a half century, not only in English but in several different languages?

Clarence "Ducky" Nash, named a Disney Legend in 1992

DISNEY QUIZ

What well-known actor and comedian has somewhat of a cameo in Disneyland's Pirates of the Caribbean attraction, as the model for a man in the scene showing a prisoner encouraging a dog to fetch him the keys to the cell?

Sid Caesar

23

May

(2005) The death on the previous day of 91-year-old Thurl Ravenscroft was announced. As a voice-over artist and singer, Ravenscroft appeared in numerous Disney films, including *101 Dalmatians, Mary Poppins,* and *The Jungle Book.* He sang bass for the Mello Men quartet, whose harmonizing can be heard most famously in *Lady and the Tramp.* "The most fun we ever had was singing barbershop for Tramp and the other dogs," Ravenscroft once said. "Walt . . . wanted them to sound like dogs, not people singing like dogs." Perhaps Ravenscroft's biggest claim to fame was growling "They're grrrrrreat!" as Tony the Tiger for Kellogg's Frosted Flakes for more than 50 years.

"The fun was there was no book to go by. You wrote the book every day. Probably the biggest strength was having a group of people who were stupid enough not to know that the things they were doing couldn't be done."

—Jack B. Lindquist, former president of Disneyland, on the theme park's early days

24
May

(1968) By joint resolution of the Congress of the United States and the House of Representatives, Walt Disney was posthumously awarded the Congressional Gold Medal, with one medal being struck for his widow, Lillian, and another for preservation at the California Institute of the Arts, which he'd founded. The resolution repeated British political cartoonist David Low's declaration (although without attribution) that Walt Disney was "the most significant figure in graphic arts since Leonardo." It also described Disneyland in Anaheim as "one of the wonders of the modern world."

DISNEY QUIZ ————————————

What schools granted Walt Disney honorary degrees?

Harvard, Yale, UCLA, and the University of Southern California

DID YOU KNOW? ————————————

The full-size steam locomotive that animator Ward Kimball had at home was one of the things that inspired Walt to use a railway as the perimeter for the Magic Kingdom.

May

(1932) One of the studios' most popular characters, Goofy, made his debut in "Mickey's Revue." And thanks to the vocal talents of gagman, story man, musician, special effects whiz, former circus clown, and future Bozo the Clown Pinto Colvig, Goofy would become a permanent member of the Disney repertory company. In "Mickey's Revue," Goofy is only an anonymous member of the audience with an unusually raucous laugh, but that idiosyncratic guffaw convinced Walt Disney that the character should be more fully developed.

BY THE NUMBERS

A winner of the *Wine Spectator* "Best of" Award of Excellence, Disney World's gourmet restaurant Victoria and Albert's has 700 vintages on its wine list.

26
May

(2000) *Shanghai Noon,* the first of a pair of East-West buddy films starring martial arts megastar Jackie Chan and dude-blond Owen Wilson, was released. A comic update on *The Wild, Wild West,* it pits Imperial Guard Chon Wang and his fast-talking, gun-toting partner Roy O'Bannon against the kidnappers of a Chinese princess and gangs of big bad gunslingers. Chon winds up as the sheriff of Nevada City, and Roy heads to New York to write pulp novels. *Shanghai Noon* turned out to be such a box office bonanza that a sequel, inevitably called *Shanghai Knights,* was released in 2003.

DID YOU KNOW? ——————

When Nikita Khrushchev almost visited Disneyland, Walt claimed he had intended to line up the eight nuclear sub-style vessels of the Submarine Voyage attraction, turn to the premier, and say, "Well, Mr. Khrushchev, here's my Disneyland submarine fleet. It's the eighth largest in the world." (The Los Angeles police chief banned the premier because of security concerns.)

May

(1933) A short cartoon featuring a song that became a Depression-era anthem for the entire country premiered. The film was "Three Little Pigs," and the song—an America-first, thumb-in-your-eye reaction to the earlier song "Brother, Can You Spare a Dime?"—was "Who's Afraid of the Big Bad Wolf?" The song was written primarily by Frank Churchill, whose other creations included "Whistle While You Work" and "Heigh-Ho" from *Snow White and the Seven Dwarfs*. Animator Fred Moore was responsible for giving the pigs, as Walt put it, "true personality." The cartoon won an Academy Award and led to three porcine sequels.

LEGENDARY PEOPLE

Who was the first woman to join Disney's WED Enterprises, responsible for creating the head of Abraham Lincoln for the New York World's Fair attraction?

Harriet Burns, named a Disney Legend in 2000

DISNEY QUIZ

What Disney property features a Lego store with an impressive Lego Loch Ness monster?

Walt Disney World's Downtown Disney Marketplace

28
May

(1966) It's a Small World, which had begun at the New York World's Fair, opened as a free-standing attraction at Disneyland. The theme song for the ten-minute ride, since duplicated at Walt Disney World in Orlando, Tokyo Disneyland, and Disneyland Paris, is by some estimates the most frequently performed song in the world. Written by Richard M. and Robert B. Sherman, the simple lyric plays continuously for the entire ride while boat passengers sweep past nearly 300 audio-animatronic dolls representing the children of the various continents and past such international landmarks as the Eiffel Tower and the Taj Mahal.

DISNEY QUIZ

Which Disney theme park has a built-in audience, with nearly 40 million people living within two hours' drive?

Tokyo Disneyland

May

(1941) A group of studio employees, led by union organizer Herb Sorrell, set up a picket line outside Disney offices. As other studios unionized, and the public assumed that *Snow White* had erased all Disney debt, employees were convinced he could pay higher wages. The dispute was exacerbated because Walt Disney, who considered employees as family, took the strike as a personal slight. To get away from it all, in August Walt left on a goodwill tour of South America. When he returned,the strike had been resolved by mediators, although loss of revenue forced him to let some employees go.

NAME THAT 'TOON

After *Sleeping Beauty* in 1959, what was Disney's next animated feature based on a fairy tale?

The Little Mermaid (1989)

30
May

(2003) *Finding Nemo,* the fifth Disney-Pixar collaboration, was released and set a Disney record for opening-weekend receipts, grossing over $70 million. Eventually it would earn $340 million domestically, its worldwide gross would reach $865 million by the end of 2004, and even its first-day DVD sales would reach $8 million. It also hit the critical jackpot, winning the Academy Award for Best Animated Feature. The film was acclaimed for its "look" as well as its story. Computer animation creates layers of underwater movement, which capture schools of fish moving at dozens of three-dimensional angles simultaneously.

DISNEY QUIZ

What other honorees received the Presidential Medal of Freedom in 1964 along with Walt Disney?

Composer Aaron Copland, former secretary of state Dean Acheson, opera diva Leontyne Price, husband and wife theater legends Alfred Lunt and Lynn Fontanne, ambassador for the disabled Helen Keller, Nobel laureate and Pulitzer Prize–winning novelist John Steinbeck, and poet Carl Sandburg

(2000) *Clerks,* a prime-time series produced by Walt Disney Television animation for Miramax Television, premiered on ABC. Its second episode, which aired June 7, was its last, making it one of Disney's least successful animated series ever. *Clerks* was based on characters from Kevin Smith's 1994 independent slacker film of the same name, famously made for $27,000. But the film's problematic humor didn't adapt well to the small screen, or to the general public.

31
May

BY THE NUMBERS

Disney World Resort employs nearly 300 certified sommeliers, or wine stewards—more than any other single company.

june

A parade on Main Street of the Magic Kingdom, 1993, in Lake Buena Vista, Florida

1

June

(1989) Typhoon Lagoon, Disney's first attempt at a combination aquatic park and thrill ride amusement park, opened at Walt Disney World in Orlando. Seven times as large as River Country, Disney World's first water park, Typhoon Lagoon came with two speed slides that each drop about 50 feet; sliders take them at about 30 mph. It also has a surf pool, where the surf comes in every 90 seconds and rises about four-and-a-half feet. One of the most intriguing areas is Shark Reef, an artificial coral reef with bonnethead and leopard sharks and tropical fish.

DISNEY QUIZ

What Disney Legend simultaneously held the number-one spots in TV ratings, movie grosses, and U.S. book sales in 1994?

Tim Allen

BY THE NUMBERS

One of the Imagineers on the technical team for the recent renovation of *The Twilight Zone* Tower of Terror estimated he rode the attraction nearly 3,000 times and often spent as much as three hours at a time strapped in while the drop sequences were tested.

June

(1989) *Dead Poets Society,* a film that earned Robin Williams an Oscar nomination for Best Actor and that launched the careers of young actors Robert Sean Leonard and Ethan Hawke, opened in limited release. It went into general circulation a week later. With a target audience of both teenagers and adults, the film made $235 million worldwide. For perhaps the first time in his career, Williams plays it unusually straight. According to legend, his character was inspired by Michael Eisner's favorite professor at Denison College. Despite being criticized as melodramatic, the screenplay by Tom Schulman won an Academy Award.

DID YOU KNOW? —————

In 1991, President George H. W. Bush presented medals to 575 Daily Points of Light honorees in a televised ceremony at the American Gardens in Epcot at Walt Disney World.

3

June

(1984) Bistro de Paris, the first "serious" restaurant at Walt Disney World, opened in the France pavilion at Epcot. Three weeks later, the gourmet restaurant Victoria and Albert's opened in the Grand Floridian Resort and Spa. These were Disney's early efforts to broaden the park's audience by playing to a mature crowd and their interest in food and wine. Eventually, led by Dieter Hannig, senior vice president of food and beverage service at Disney World, Disney would boast a dozen first-class restaurants, including Jiko at the Animal Kingdom Lodge and Todd English's Bluezoo at the Dolphin Hotel, along with a brewpub and a half-dozen notable wine lists.

DISNEY QUIZ

To whom is the castle at Disneyland Paris dedicated?

Sleeping Beauty, or "La Belle au Bois Dormant"

4
June

(1990) The Walt Disney World Dolphin Hotel opened, completing a two-hotel complex near Epcot that also included the six-month-old Swan Hotel. Architectural iconoclast Michael Graves designed both hotels, which are lightheartedly capped with huge statues of the water creatures from which they take their names. Then-CEO Michael Eisner was delighted when Graves's proposed models showed a postmodern fountain-topped pyramid for the first hotel and a play on the classic vault for the other. Told to "lighten them up" further, Graves added the playful animals and chose the beachy turquoise and stucco. Visible from the highway, the hotels have become attractions in themselves.

LEGENDARY PEOPLE

What performer was such a staple figure of the Golden Horseshoe Revue at Disneyland, beginning in 1955, that he earned a place in *The Guinness Book of World Records* for most performances of a show?

Wally Boag, named a Disney Legend in 1995

5

June

(1995) Plans for Disney's Animal Kingdom were announced. A seamless combination of amusement park and wildlife preserve covering 500 acres and housing some 200 species of animals, it revolutionized zoological parks when it opened in April 1998. The park has three areas—Asia, Africa, and DinoLand—with a fourth as yet unspecified area rumored to become a kingdom of mythological animals. The park's hub is the Tree of Life, a concrete-covered oil derrick that stands 145 feet tall, has branches 170 feet across, and is covered with carvings of 350 animals whose outlines flow into one another like a puzzle.

DID YOU KNOW?

While Walt Disney and his staff were trying to integrate sound into the first Mickey Mouse cartoons, a test sequence was screened for the employees' wives and girlfriends while Walt, Ub Iwerks, and others played whistles, harmonicas, and cowbells. Though the women were lukewarm on the project, the animators continued and produced "Steamboat Willie" in 1928.

6
June

(1944) On a different sort of D day, Mickey Mouse played one of the greatest, if invisible, roles of his career: he served as the password for American troops during the Normandy invasion. It was only fair: Walt Disney and his staff had made scores of propaganda and educational and even technical films for the government since right after the Pearl Harbor attack. Mickey, Donald, and other Disney characters also served as mascots and emblems for armed-services brigades and companies throughout the war, although in truth, Mickey was used on fewer insignias than his blustering duck buddy.

DISNEY QUIZ

What beloved child actress performed the dedication of Sleeping Beauty Castle when it opened at Disneyland in 1957?

Shirley Temple

NAME THAT 'TOON

During the production of what cartoon did animator Fred Moore develop the "squash and stretch" technique, which made characters' bodies and feet extend and deflate while walking—and which became a popular way to express a character's personality?

"Three Little Pigs"

June

(1987) The annual convention of the American Association of Museums opened in San Francisco. At one seminar, called "Education versus Entertainment: Competing for Audiences," Imagineering chief Marty Sklar relayed "Mickey's Ten Commandments," distilled from years of talking with Walt Disney about his vision: (1) Know your audience; (2) Wear your guest's shoes; (3) Organize the flow of people and ideas; (4) Create a "weenie," or visual hook; (5) Communicate with visual literacy; (6) Avoid overload; (7) Tell one story at a time; (8) Avoid contradiction; (9) For every ounce of treatment, provide a ton of fun; and (10) Keep it up.

BY THE NUMBERS

At the height of *The Mickey Mouse Club* show's popularity, the Mickey Mouse Club ears sold at a rate of **24,000** a day.

8

June

(1902) The infant Walt Disney was baptized at the St. Paul Congregational Church on Chicago's Tripp Avenue. His parents were extremely devout; his mother, Flora, played the church's organ, which his father, Elias, had helped build. Walt Disney absorbed much of his family's religious beliefs, although he and his brother Roy were later disenchanted by what they saw as their father's growing greed and the sanctimony of many churchgoers. Disney did not belong to any specific religious group as an adult.

DISNEY QUIZ ————————————————

What was the nickname of singer Cliff Edwards, who voiced Jiminy Cricket in various Disney productions?

Ukulele Ike, who specialized in what he called "effin'," a half-humming technique that sounded like a Jews' harp

BY THE NUMBERS ————————————————

The high-powered Rock 'n' Roller Coaster Starring Aerosmith begins with a vertical leap of 80 feet at a force that equals that of an F-14, approximately five times the force of gravity.

(1934) Donald Duck, a feisty salt of a squawker who became an unexpected American hero, made his first appearance in a cartoon. Unlike most Disney characters, Donald was not introduced as a guest star in a Mickey Mouse cartoon. He first appeared as a supporting character in a "Silly Symphony" film called "The Wise Little Hen." Donald immediately caught the public eye, and within a couple of years the cover phrase "A Mickey Mouse cartoon" wasn't even applied to him. His popularity ultimately exceeded Mickey's, though he never really became a corporate symbol.

9
June

DID YOU KNOW?

When *Apollo 8* made it to the moon in 1968, German scientist Wernher von Braun reportedly called Disney animator Ward Kimball, with whom he collaborated on the three-part Disney series on space travel in the 1950s, and said, "Well, Ward, it looks as though they are following our script."

10
June

(1995) *Pocahontas* premiered in a rare outdoor setting, New York's Central Park, before an estimated crowd of 110,000. The movie went into general release a week later. Disney animators and artists made repeated visits to the Jamestown settlement in Virginia and researched the colonial period extensively; they also consulted with American Indian scholars and storytellers about the Powhatan culture. The film's history is not so authentic, however, when it suggests a romance between Pocahontas and Capt. John Smith: at the time, she was likely only a young girl, probably nine or ten years old, while he was a veteran explorer.

NAME THAT 'TOON —————————————

In what animated short does Walt Disney appear in caricature as a matador, with the film's chief animator Ward Kimball as his servant?

"Ferdinand the Bull" (1938)

DISNEY QUIZ —————————————

What world-famous architectural landmark heavily influenced Herb Ryman's design for Sleeping Beauty Castle at Disneyland?

Neuschwanstein Castle in Bavaria, one of "Mad King" Ludwig's creations

11

June

(1928) "Poor Papa," the first short film starring Oswald the Lucky Rabbit, Walt Disney's first popular cartoon character, was finally released. (Like the Mickey Mouse of "Plane Crazy," the original Oswald drawn was not the one audiences met first: "Trolley Troubles," which was made after "Poor Papa," was released the year before.)

The cheerful but spunky Oswald appeared in 26 shorts between 1927 and 1928. He was inspired by distributor Charles Mintz, who had married "Alice" distributor Margaret Winkler, who heard that Universal Studios wanted a series featuring a rabbit. Oswald had a round head and button nose, big black eyes, and white gloves and shoes—clearly a Walt Disney creation. The series was popular, but when Walt asked Mintz for a raise, he learned that Mintz owned the rights to the character. Walt quit on the spot.

DID YOU KNOW?

Not only was the original *Love Bug* movie a surprise hit for Disney, it was also the best free publicity Volkswagen could ever have wished for. Ten days after the film was released, on March 23, 1969, a line of 100 Volkswagen Beetles paraded down Disneyland's Main Street.

12
June

(1999) *Tarzan* had its world premiere at the El Capitan Theater in Los Angeles. One of Disney's most successful non-Pixar collaborations, it grossed more than $450 million worldwide. "You'll Be in My Heart," written by Phil Collins for the film, not only won an Oscar for Best Song but became a number-one hit. The sweep of Tarzan's movement through the jungle was partly modeled on the motions of skaters and boarders. Tarzan's swinging segments were made using a digital technique known as "Deep Canvas," which garnered the studios a technical Academy Award.

DID YOU KNOW?

In *Bedknobs and Broomsticks* (1971), the armor that is magically animated by Miss Price had originally been assembled for the Charlton Heston epic *El Cid,* filmed on location in Spain in 1960 and 1961; the armor was shipped back to the United States for the musical film *Camelot* in 1967 and then borrowed again for *B&B.*

(1925) Walt Disney proposed to Lillian Marie Bounds. Lilly met Walt after she got a job filling in cels (the celluloid sheets used in animation) at the Disney studios for $15 a week. Walt had previously displayed little interest in women, and he proposed to Lilly by asking whether she'd rather he buy a new car for the both of them or an engagement ring for her. "He seemed quite disappointed I didn't let him buy the car," she told her daughter Diane years later. The two were married in July.

13
June

LEGENDARY PEOPLE

What special effects wiz had the idea to project a moving face onto a bust to make it seem to come alive in the Haunted Mansion attraction?

Yale Gracey, named a Disney Legend in 1999

DISNEY QUIZ

What former Mouseketeer played Mark McCain, son of TV *Rifleman* Chuck Connors, from 1958 to 1961?

Johnny Crawford

14

June

(1959) The Disneyland monorail, the first daily-operated monorail in the country, made its first official run on a 0.8-mile track circling Tomorrowland. The Disneyland monorail was originally conceived as an amusement ride. In 1961, it was extended to the Disneyland Hotel, where it became a transportation vehicle.

On the same day, Disneyland's Submarine Voyage attraction, with a fleet of eight vessels named after U.S. nuclear submarines, was officially dedicated. Riding in one of the ships—including *Nautilus*, Captain Nemo's vessel in *20,000 Leagues under the Sea*—guests saw such fantastical spectacles as a giant sea serpent and the lost city of Atlantis.

DID YOU KNOW?

For *Bedknobs and Broomsticks,* instead of filming the Portobello Road sequence in London's famous antiques row, Disney staffers built a three-block replica and filled the stands with period merchandise and 200 "shoppers." According to Dave Smith, this crowd included "veterans of music halls, vaudeville, rep shows, radio, silent films, and early talkies."

(1994) *The Lion King,* one of the most successful films in the studios' history, premiered in New York and Los Angeles before going into general release a week later. The release was boosted by a televised concert featuring Elton John, who cowrote several songs for the soundtrack—which earned $1 billion by itself. Not only did John and Tim Rice win the Academy Award for Best Song, for "Can You Feel the Love Tonight," but Hans Zimmer, who wrote the background soundtrack, also got an Oscar. The film alone grossed $1 billion and inspired one of Broadway's biggest stage shows.

15
June

BY THE NUMBERS

In 1989, a single cel from the original black-and-white version of the cartoon "Orphan's Benefit" (1934) sold at auction for $286,000.

DISNEY QUIZ

At what Disney park will you find a Hollywood-style walk of fame, with handprint replicas and autographs of the stars?

Disney-MGM Studios, at the replica of Grauman's Chinese Theatre

16
June

(1934) "Mickey's Steam-Roller," the only cartoon to costar Mickey's nephews—Morty and Ferdy Fieldmouse, the children of Mickey's sister Amelia—was released. Morty and Ferdy (whose named was sometimes spelled "Ferdie") usually appeared in cartoon books and were regulars in the Mickey Mouse comic strip then being drawn by Floyd Gottfredson. The nephews made their first appearance in the syndicated strip in September 1932, so they were familiar to fans when "Steam-Roller" came out. In the cartoon, Mickey is pitching his usual woo to Minnie when the mischievous pair crawls into the machine and it takes off, eventually crashing into a hotel.

DISNEY QUIZ

Which Mouseketeer from the original *Mickey Mouse Club* later wrote a book called *Walt, Mickey and Me* about his experiences?

Paul Petersen

June

(2002) The company launched a special auction of Elvis Presley memorabilia to publicize the imminent premiere of its animated film *Lilo and Stitch*. The film's soundtrack featured six original tracks by Presley—several of which inspire the title characters to terpsichorean extremes—and a new version of "Burning Love," recorded for the movie by Wynonna Judd. Among the items up for auction, which took place on eBay until July 4, were two of Presley's costume scarves.

(2003) An exhibit called "Designing Disney's Theme Parks: Architects of Reassurance" opened at the prestigious Canadian Center for Architecture in Montreal.

WHERE'S MICKEY?

In 2005, Mickey served as grand marshal of the Tournament of Roses Parade in Pasadena, California, part of the Disney Company's worldwide advertising campaign for Disneyland's 50th-birthday celebration.

18
June

(1996) The first family moved into Celebration, the town that Disney built and marketed as "a place that takes you back to the age of innocence." New Urbanism advocate Robert A. M. Stern designed the planned community, famous for its pastel houses, public spaces, and some intentionally old-fashioned traditions, such as "snow" blown from bubble machines mounted on lampposts during the holidays. Following its original plan, the Disney Company put Celebration on the market in 2003, and by the next year it had been sold to a private real estate investment group for a reported $42.3 million.

DISNEY QUIZ

What Disney Company executive almost realized his goal to climb the highest mountain on each of the seven continents, scaling six of those mountains but failing twice to reach the top of Mount Everest?

The late Frank Wells, former president of the Walt Disney Company

(1996) The hunchback of Notre Dame was the star of a premiere party in an unlikely spot for a supposedly athletically challenged hero, the Superdome in New Orleans. He was also celebrated by a parade through the French Quarter. The film went into general release two days later.

19
June

(1998) *Mulan* went into general release after a premiere at the Hollywood Bowl on June 5. It was the first animated feature to have been primarily produced at the Features Animation facility at Walt Disney World in Orlando.

DID YOU KNOW?

In the 1975 movie *Escape to Witch Mountain,* the mansion used as Xanthus is not a set, but a real castle near Pebble Beach that was built by Templeton Crocker in the late 1920s and early 1930s at a cost of $3 million; he used pieces of lava he collected from Mount Vesuvius and physical souvenirs from Europe to construct a replica of a Byzantine palace.

20

June

(1976) River Country, Disney's first aquatic park, opened at Walt Disney World in Orlando. Conceived as a nostalgic Tom Sawyer attraction, River Country featured rope swings, a "white-water" raft ride, white sand beaches, and a 330,000-gallon swimming hole. Even after the construction of the more modern aquatic parks Typhoon Lagoon and Blizzard Beach, with their speed slides and surf pools, River Country remained popular among fans of the quieter life. However, the crowds gradually diminished, and Disney closed the park in September 2001, initially saying it might later be reopened. In 2004, they confirmed that River Country had run its course.

NAME THAT 'TOON

In a December 2001 *Billboard* magazine poll, what Disney animated classic was named the fifth most popular video of all time?

Snow White and the Seven Dwarfs

DISNEY QUIZ

What Disney creation did *Time* magazine name one of the most important inventions of 2003?

Lucky the Dinosaur, the first-ever free-roaming audio-animatronic creature

(2002) *Lilo and Stitch,* a film trumpeted as a return to old-fashioned hand animation, was released. It was Disney's most successful animated film since *The Lion King. Lilo* presents a clever twist on the classic boy-and-his-dog story: a girl and her alien. It also resembles another Disney classic, *Pinocchio,* in that the nonhuman eventually becomes more "human" by showing a loving heart. Artistically, *Lilo and Stitch* has a retro Disney look, gaining much of its atmospheric power through bright watercolors and simple, flowing backgrounds. The film's success was followed by a video sequel, *Stitch!,* and the usual television series.

21
June

> *"I have watched constantly that in our movie work the highest moral and spiritual standards are upheld, whether it deals with fables or with stories of living actions. Whatever success I have had in bringing clean, informative entertainment to people of all ages, I attribute in great part to my Congregational upbringing and my lifelong habit of prayer."*
>
> —Walt Disney, in an essay for the book **Faith Is a Star** (1963)

June

(1988) A day after its celebrity premiere at Radio City Music Hall in New York, *Who Framed Roger Rabbit* opened around the country. Its exhilarating interaction of live and animated characters, and of real and cartoon worlds, made it a huge success and earned it four Academy Awards (the most since *Mary Poppins* in 1964), including an award for special achievement in animation direction. The movie's $30 million budget was the largest ever approved for an animated feature, but even so, it eventually cost close to $50 million. Fortunately, it grossed three times that.

DID YOU KNOW?

"Ubbe Iwwerks," the original Dutch spelling of animator Ub Iwerks's name, appears in a joke on Disney World's Main Street: a sign for an optometrist's office that makes passersby believe they're seeing double.

June

(1963) The Enchanted Tiki Room opened at Disneyland, becoming the first attraction to have sophisticated audio-animatronic creatures capable of performing on their own. More than 400 audio-animatronic animals and things—birds, plants, tiki masks, and carved tiki poles—take part in the act. It's said that the Enchanted Tiki Room was one of Walt's favorite attractions, if not his very favorite. Although the music all sounds authentic, it was written by the Sherman brothers, so in addition to "It's a Small World," they bear responsibility for "In the Tiki, Tiki, Tiki, Tiki, Tiki Room."

DISNEY QUIZ

What original Mouseketeer went on to play middle son Robbie Douglas on the TV show *My Three Sons* from 1960 to 1971?

Don Agrati, who changed his name to Don Grady

BY THE NUMBERS

Since its founding in 1995, the Disney Wildlife Conservation Fund, which sponsors global programs for the study and protection of animals and ecosystems, has awarded more than $8 million to non-profit groups.

24

June

(1893) Roy Oliver Disney, the third of four brothers, was born in Chicago. Roy began looking out for the younger Walt early on. Roy got Walt a job at Kansas City Slides, let Walt live in his apartment, and put his own engagement on hold to get the studios started. Roy usually had to find the money for Walt's dreams, convincing bankers to go along while his family as well as Walt's bordered on bankruptcy. When Walt died in 1966, Roy had been about to retire. Instead, he took charge of promoting, funding, and developing Walt Disney World. Roy dedicated Disney World to his brother at its opening in October 1971 and died two months later.

LEGENDARY PEOPLE

What young star of the "Alice" shorts, Disney's first series, left Disney in 1925, believing—incorrectly, as it turned out—that she could get a much more lucrative deal with one of the major studios?

Virginia Davis, named a Disney Legend in 1998

(2005) John Fiedler, the voice of Piglet in Disney's Winnie-the-Pooh films, died at age 80, one day after Paul Winchell, the voice of Tigger, died at age 82. Fiedler's movie credits included *12 Angry Men,* as well as the Disney classics *The Fox and the Hound* and *The Rescuers.* Winchell was best known as ventriloquist to dummy Jerry Mahoney, but he also played Boomer in *The Fox and the Hound* and the Chinese cat in *The Aristocats.*

One month later, blues legend Long John Baldry, who had a second career as a voice actor and narrated Winnie-the-Pooh albums for the Disney Company, also died.

25
June

DID YOU KNOW?

For many years, the restaurant inside Cinderella Castle at Walt Disney World was named King Stefan's Banquet Hall, which was sort of a puzzle, since Stefan is Sleeping Beauty's father, not Cinderella's. Stefan was finally booted off the title in 1997.

June

(1929) "Mickey's Follies," a sort of barnyard revue, introduced the love song that became Mickey's theme. After some uncertainty in earlier cartoons, the song "Minnie's Yoo Hoo" made it clear that Minnie would be Mickey's permanent companion. Walt Disney wrote the lyrics to "Minnie's Yoo Hoo," and Carl Stalling supplied the tune. The song began, "I'm the guy they call little Mickey Mouse, / Got a sweetie down in the chicken house." That "sweetie" is "neither fat nor skinny, / She's my little Minnie Mouse." The ditty became the theme song for the original Mickey Mouse Club.

DISNEY QUIZ

Which Mouseketeer from the original series became the featured dancer on *The Lawrence Welk Show* for more than two decades, from 1961 to 1983?

Bobby Burgess

NAME THAT 'TOON

According to Disney archivist Dave Smith, for what cartoon did the animation department come up with transparent paint to ink in ghosts?

"Lonesome Ghosts" (1937)

June

(**1997**) Following a sneak preview on June 14 at the New Amsterdam Theater in New York City, *Hercules* went into general release. The film was fairly well reviewed and warmly enough received, but because of its high cost— $179 million, $100 million of it attributed to "artist labor" (the film involved nearly 700 artists, and animation took two years)—it earned only about $30 million. Following its release, the Paris animation studio was shut down. With many visually striking scenes, however, *Hercules* featured the first use in animation of morphing, Pain and Panic being shape shifters.

BY THE NUMBERS

At 17 minutes long and $17 million in costs, the "Captain Eo" attraction starring Michael Jackson, produced by George Lucas, and directed by Francis Ford Coppola set a record in the mid-1980s as minute for minute the most expensive Hollywood film ever.

June

(2003) *Pirates of the Caribbean: The Curse of the Black Pearl* had its grand premiere at Disneyland, as a salute to the attraction that inspired it. The film would gross more than $300 million in the United States, and $650 million worldwide. And it would earn star Johnny Depp a surprising Oscar nomination for Best Actor. Although it was only nominally inspired by the theme park attraction, *Pirates* follows the Imagineering tradition of saluting its antecedents. The ride's theme song, "Yo Ho, A Pirate's Life for Me," is heard several times in the film, for instance.

"Although I may not qualify as Walt Disney's best friend, a colorless thing for a wife to be, anyway, I am sure I [qualify] as his severest critic. I always look on the dark side."

—Lillian Disney

(1935) "Who Killed Cock Robin?," a "Silly Symphony" based on the old rhyme, was released. Featuring a clever transformation of Mae West as Jenny Wren, it was part of Disney animators' growing fondness for caricature. As early as "Mickey's Gala Premiere" (1933), Mickey dreams that he is the lead in a movie whose opening is attended by Clark Gable, Charlie Chaplin, Greta Garbo, Laurel and Hardy, and Marlene Dietrich. And in "Broken Toys," also in 1935, the animators had used caricatures of stars such as W. C. Fields to add another layer of jokes.

29
June

DISNEY QUIZ

How did architect Frank Gehry honor Lillian Disney in his design of the Walt Disney Concert Hall in Los Angeles, for which she donated more than $50 million?

To recognize her love of flowers, he designed a floral pattern for the upholstery which he named "Lillian," and he designed a rose-petal fountain in the garden, covered in broken delft china, titled "A Rose for Lilly."

30
June

(1993) The company announced it would buy Miramax Film Corp. from its founders, brothers Harvey and Bob Weinstein, for about $80 million, with the Weinsteins staying on to run the studio for Disney. Disney chairman Michael Eisner and then-CEO Frank Wells believed Miramax was the perfect vehicle to broaden the Disney brand into the hip indie market, and the unexpected success of *Pulp Fiction,* made for $8 million and earning more than $200 worldwide, seemed to prove them right. But in 2004, after a series of philosophical and financial differences, the Disney Company decided not to renew the Weinsteins' contracts.

NAME THAT 'TOON————————

What early Mickey Mouse cartoon parodied a popular 1927 silent film starring Douglas Fairbanks called *The Gaucho?*

"Gallopin' Gaucho" (1928)

july

Fantasyland at Disneyland in Anaheim, California, 1955

1

July

(1932) Walt Disney signed Herman "Kay" Kamen to a contract, putting him in charge of merchandise sales. It was to be a lucrative decision, because although there had been some very limited Mickey licensing before, it had not been closely controlled. Among Kamen's successes were the Mickey Mouse watch, which would have been a career maker by itself; an agreement with the Gund company, manufacturers of the famous bears, to market plush versions of Disney characters from 1947 to 1971; and International Silver cups and silverware, including the Mickey Mouse spoon, one of the most popular "box top" premiums of the 1930s.

DID YOU KNOW? ——————————

After Ron and Diane Disney Miller named their first child Christopher and then had three daughters, Diane's dad began to complain that none of the grandchildren shared his name. When the Millers' fifth child was born, he was happily christened Walter Elias Disney Miller.

(1986) *The Great Mouse Detective,* an animated Sherlock Holmes story, was released. Based on a popular children's book, *Basil of Baker Street* by Eve Titus, the story stars a mouse named Basil, after the great movie *Holmes, Basil Rathbone.* Henry Mancini wrote the score and two songs; Melissa Manchester wrote and sang the third.

2
July

(1964) *The Moon-Spinners,* based on Mary Stewart's mystery and starring Hayley Mills in her fifth Disney film in four years, was released. It features veteran actresses who would have frightened any youngster who hadn't (as Mills fortunately had) grown up in the business: Joan Greenwood, Irene Papas, and silent-film idol Pola Negri.

LEGENDARY PEOPLE

Although better known for his role in the Disney Davy Crockett TV series and films, who was hired by Walt Disney in 1951 to dance on camera and serve as a model for the company's audio-animatronics technology?

Buddy Ebsen, named a Disney Legend in 1993

3
July

(1914) George Bruns, who would win four Best Song Academy Awards for his work at Disney, was born in Oregon. His most famous creation was "The Ballad of Davy Crockett," which spent four months at the top of the Hit Parade and sold seven million copies in the first five months. Bruns also wrote "The Bare Necessities" from *The Jungle Book* and "Yo Ho, A Pirate's Life for Me," written for the Pirates of the Caribbean attraction and used again in the movie. Altogether, Bruns scored more than 100 movies and TV shows.

(1910) Marcellite Garner, a staffer in the ink-and-paint department who became the first voice of Minnie Mouse, was born. She died in 1993.

BY THE NUMBERS

Within a few weeks of the 1954 premiere of Disney's *Davy Crockett* TV series, more than ten million coonskin caps had been sold.

(2005) The Fourth of July fireworks display was one of the biggest in history, involving 1,600 shells, more than twice as many as the regular nightly "Wishes" program.

(1862) Oxford professor Charles Lutwidge Dodgson took the three young daughters of his friend Henry Liddell rowing. Alice, age ten, asked Dodgson to write down the stories he had told them about a little girl exploring a magical realm where animals talk. Two years later, Dodgson published *Alice's Adventures Underground,* under the name Lewis Carroll. Walt Disney's first series of shorts was a twist on Wonderland, in which he launched a real-life Alice into animated situations.

4
July

NAME THAT 'TOON

What feature film's overall look was influenced by the fluid flow of Arabian calligraphy and the swirl of Persian art and design?

Aladdin

DISNEY QUIZ

What son of a famous actor was fired after a short stint as a Mouseketeer on the original *Mickey Mouse Club?*

Mickey Rooney Jr.

5
July

(1988) Maelstrom, the water-ride attraction in the Norway pavilion at Epcot's World Showcase, opened. It remains the only thrill ride in the World Showcase, although it's a moderate one. Riding in Viking-like boats, guests coast through a panorama of scenes from medieval Norwegian history until a trio of trolls cast a curse on the crowd and send the boats out of control. Although Maelstrom is the only one with much action, Epcot has two other water rides: the soporific El Rio del Tiempo in the Mexico pavilion and the more educational Living with the Land at The Land in Future World.

NAME THAT 'TOON————————————

What is the title of the TV series, which ran on the Disney Channel and ABC between 1992 and 1996, that stars Goofy as a suburban single father?

Goof Troop

6

July

(1918) Sebastian Cabot, the portly actor whose plush voice and precise accent made him seem the quintessential British gentleman—but who was surprisingly a Cockney—was born in London. Famous as Mr. French on *A Family Affair,* Cabot became a sought-after voice actor. In 1963, he narrated Disney's *The Sword in the Stone.* In 1966, Cabot recorded the narration for "Winnie the Pooh and the Honey Tree," which found instant success and inspired several sequels. In 1967, he voiced Bagheera the panther, Mowgli's protector. He also appeared in or narrated several live-action Disney films and TV shows.

"Once a man has tasted freedom, he will never be content to be a slave. That is why I believe that this frightfulness we see everywhere today is only temporary. Tomorrow will be better for as long as America keeps alive the ideals of freedom and a better life. . . . I thank God and America for the right to live and raise my family under the flag of tolerance, democracy, and freedom."

—Disney CEO Michael Eisner in a statement responding to the 9/11 attacks, quoting a speech Walt Disney gave during the intermission of a Metropolitan Opera broadcast after Pearl Harbor Day in 1941

July

(1963) *Summer Magic,* which was mostly a vehicle for Hayley Mills but is remembered for Burl Ives's rendition of the "Ugly Bug Ball" song written by Richard and Robert Sherman, was released. *Summer Magic* is a version of Kate Douglas Wiggin's novel *Mother Carey's Chickens,* which was published in 1911 and had been made into a movie once before, in 1938.

(1971) Walt Disney's first partner, Ub Iwerks, died in Burbank. Even though he and Walt had long been estranged, his contribution to the company earned him one of the Imagineers' highest compliments, a pretend business sign along Disney World's Main Street.

NAME THAT 'TOON

What Disney-produced war short shows Donald Duck as an ordinary American who's reluctant to turn his paycheck over to the IRS and thus becomes the subject of a tug-of-war, at first conversational and then literal, between a thrifty Scots duck (an early version of Uncle Scrooge McDuck) and a zoot-suited spendthrift?

"The Spirit of '43"

8
July

(2005) The company announced a truce with former animation head Roy E. Disney and dissident investor Stanley Gold after an acrimonious two-year battle. The statement reported that Roy Disney would return to the Disney Company as director emeritus. In return, Disney and Gold, instigators of the shareholders revolt against then-CEO Michael Eisner and his supporters on the board of directors, said they would not nominate a slate of rival candidates for the board but would accept the company's. They agreed to drop a lawsuit challenging the selection of Robert Iger as Eisner's successor and said they would submit no shareholder resolutions or petitions for at least five years.

DISNEY QUIZ

Who supplied the distinctive voice of Slinky Dog in *Toy Story* and *Toy Story 2*?

Jim Varney, best known as the silly star of Disney's *Ernest* movies

9
July

(1999) *Tarzan Rocks!*, an elaborate stage musical based on the hit animated film, featuring Phil Collins's Oscar-winning radio hits and incorporating elements of street-blading stunts and even Cirque du Soleil–style acrobatics, officially opened in DinoLand at Disney's Animal Kingdom. *Tarzan Rocks!* has a chorus of in-line skaters, dressed as apes, who speed through the audience and perform a series of flips and ramp jumps on stage. To dramatize Tarzan's skill in swinging from vines, the show also borrows rope-gymnastics moves from modern-day aerialists for an aboveground pas de deux between Tarzan and Jane. A full-scale theatrical production of *Tarzan* opened on Broadway in 2006.

LEGENDARY PEOPLE —————————————

What young British actress provided the voices for two of Disney's sweetest animated heroines, Alice in *Alice in Wonderland* (1951) and Wendy Darling in *Peter Pan* (1953)?

Kathryn Beaumont, named a Disney Legend in 1998

10
July

(1981) *The Fox and the Hound,* which marked the end of one animation era and the beginning of another, was released after nearly four years in production. Despite its checkered departure of a dozen animators, headed by Don Bluth, in 1979 interrupted its progress—it was an enormous success. Veteran animators Frank Thomas and Ollie Johnston, aka "Frank 'n' Ollie," were responsible for much of the early work. But after the Bluth mutiny, the animation was produced by younger staffers such as Glen Keane, Andy Gaskill, Ron Clements, and John Musker, a new generation who spearheaded a more modern Disney style.

DISNEY QUIZ

What dominates the second floor of the World of Disney Store in Manhattan?

A build-your-own Mr. Potato Head area

BY THE NUMBERS

After being ousted from his position as Disney president in 1996, Michael Ovitz reportedly received a settlement of $140 million—$10 million per month of employment.

11
July

(1991) The Walt Disney Company and Pixar Animation Studios announced that they would share the costs of Pixar's first feature film using its proprietary computer-animation techniques. This marked the start of a phenomenally profitable partnership. In 1997, after the success of that first film, *Toy Story*, the partnership was strengthened: Disney and Pixar would release at least five films together—*Toy Story* and *Toy Story 2, A Bug's Life, Finding Nemo,* and *Monsters, Inc.*—which would generate more than $2.5 billion worldwide. After more than a year of back-and-forth negotiations, the Disney Company bought Pixar for more than $7 billion in 2006 and elevated Pixar founder Steve Jobs to the Disney board of directors.

DID YOU KNOW? ——————

After the Walt Disney Concert Hall in Los Angeles opened in 2003, the building's stainless steel surfaces reflected beams of light so bright they made the sidewalk sizzle, sunburned passersby, and sent nearby condo residents' air-conditioning bills soaring. So in 2005, the Los Angeles County Board of Supervisors ordered that the panels be hand-sanded down to a duller surface. The sanding cost about $90,000.

July

(2005) It was announced that Disneyland would be the first corporate entity, rather than an entertainer or group, to be given a sidewalk star along the Walk of Fame in Hollywood. This was just the latest in the company's constellation, which includes stars for Mickey Mouse, Walt Disney, his brother Roy, Snow White, and Donald Duck. The Disneyland star is next to, rather than on, the traditional Walkway, in the entrance to Disney's Soda Fountain and Studio Store. The store adjoins the historic El Capitan Theatre on Hollywood Boulevard, which the Disney Company restored.

DID YOU KNOW?

The castle at Tokyo Disneyland is a copy of Disney World's Cinderella Castle, while the one in Hong Kong is a duplicate of Sleeping Beauty Castle at Disneyland.

13

July

(1925) Only 18 months after beginning work at the Disney studios as an inker and painter, Lillian Bounds married Walt Disney at her brother's home in Idaho. Lillian was a shrewd partner to the headstrong artist. She needed to be, with the Disney brothers so close to ruin so many times over the years. She quit work at the studios after she married; but in 1927, during the crisis that followed the discovery of Oswald's ownership, she returned to filling in cels. Lillian remarried after Walt's death, but she continued to use the last name Disney until she died in 1997.

DISNEY QUIZ ————————————

What made-for-TV Disney movie included an appearance by actress Butterfly McQueen of *Gone with the Wind* fame?

Polly (1989), a musical version of the *Pollyanna* story

"These virtual reality games the children are playing with—I told them we were doing this 40 years ago! Disneyland is virtual reality."

—John Hench, longtime Disney Imagineer

14

July

(1981) The first *Walt Disney's World on Ice* show premiered in East Rutherford, New Jersey. Actually produced by Irvin and Kenneth Feld of Ringling Bros. and Barnum & Bailey, it re-created classic Disney stories and musical numbers via the increasingly popular sport of figure skating. The first troupe toured 20 cities. Every year since, a new live touring production has been mounted, often reprising or even promoting a specific Disney theme or release: *Beauty and the Beast, Aladdin, Peter Pan, Snow White and the Seven Dwarfs,* and so on.

WHERE'S MICKEY?

In 1935, a published report in the *American Exporter* counted 80 licenses of Mickey merchandise in the United States, 15 in Canada, 40 in England, 80 on the European continent, and 15 in Australia. The *New York Telegraph* estimated Disney's total sales for that year would top $35 million.

15
July

(1995) The glass-sided Fairy-Tale Wedding Pavilion opened at Walt Disney World in Orlando. It remains the most popular wedding venue in the park. The pavilion, which occupies its own private island between the Grand Floridian and Polynesian resorts, is the centerpiece of Disney's highly successful Fairy Tale Weddings division. Cinderella Castle is directly across Seven Seas Lagoon from the chapel and rises romantically in the window over the altar. Cinderella's coach can transport the bride to the Magic Kingdom if she desires, but the palm-heavy solarium is a major reception venue.

BY THE NUMBERS ————————————————

At the height of its popularity, it was estimated that three-quarters of the TV sets in the United States were tuned to the original *Mickey Mouse Club* show.

16
July

(1954) Walt Disney presided over the groundbreaking ceremonies for Disneyland in Anaheim, California. It had been more of a struggle than anyone knew, especially between Walt and brother Roy, who believed the project would bankrupt the studio. Walt sold his Palm Springs vacation home, cashed in his life insurance, and borrowed from his own employees while pushing the project. Reluctantly, Roy Disney took the park proposal to possible network sponsors. The clinching funds finally came from ABC: in return for a half million in cash and another $450,000 in guarantees, ABC would get a one-third share of the new park and a weekly television series.

DISNEY QUIZ

According to the Cinderella Princess Court, an hour-long interactive event that is the singular attraction of New York City's World of Disney Store, what are the four "princess principles"?

Wisdom, grace, kindness, and honesty

NAME THAT 'TOON

What animated short served as the debut vehicle for Donald's ducky girlfriend, then named Donna and only later renamed Daisy?

"Don Donald" (1937)

July

(1989) Splash Mountain, one of the most popular attractions at Disneyland and the first theme park ride to rely on a computer to control the motion, opened. At the time, the 52-foot flume was the longest in the world. The back story of the attraction was based on the Disney film *Song of the South*, and many of the more than 100 audio-animatronic characters, including Brer Rabbit and Brer Fox, came from Uncle Remus stories. Exactly three years later, on July 17, 1992, a second Splash Mountain opened at Walt Disney World, and shortly thereafter another version opened in Tokyo.

DISNEY QUIZ ————————————

What animated villain did Walt Disney describe as a cross between Lady Macbeth and the Big Bad Wolf?

The evil queen and her wicked witch alter ego in *Snow White*, both created by Joe Grant

(1955) Almost exactly one year after construction began, Disneyland in Anaheim opened to the public for the first time. The park comprised five themed "lands" and 20 attractions on 160 acres, and had cost $17 million—a price that only a few years later would scarcely cover the creation of a major thrill ride (Big Thunder Mountain) or high-tech attraction (Captain EO). Approximately 50,000 visitors paid $1 each to enter the magic kingdom. In less than two months, Disneyland welcomed its millionth guest.

18
July

DID YOU KNOW?

The list of famous alums of the *MMC*, the third *Mickey Mouse Club* series, includes Britney Spears; Justin Timberlake; Christina Aguilera; J. C. Chasez; T. J. Fantini; Tiffini Hale and the four other members of the music group The Party; Jason Minor and Jason Carson of the Nashville band Shiloh; Rhona Bennett, a later addition to En Vogue; *Felicity*'s Keri Russell; and Ryan Gosling of *Young Hercules*.

19

July

(1999) The Carolwood Pacific Historical Society, supported by the Walt Disney Family Foundation, dedicated the Walt Disney Barn, containing his *Lilly Belle* engine, in Griffith Park in Los Angeles. Having loved railroads since his first summer job, at age 15, on the Atchison, Topeka, and Santa Fe Railroad, Walt's lifelong hobby was the Carolwood-Pacific Railway, named for the street in the Los Angeles neighborhood of Holmby Hills where he and Lilly bought a home in 1948. There he built a one-eighth-scale steam engine whose track included a 46-foot loop, an elevated berm, and a 90-foot tunnel that went under Lilly's flower beds. The barn is open on the third Sunday of each month, and more than 10,000 Disney fans have visited.

LEGENDARY PEOPLE ————

What stage actress's performance in *Camelot* on Broadway in the early 1960s inspired Walt Disney suddenly to go backstage and offer her a part in his upcoming movie musical *Mary Poppins*?

Julie Andrews, named a Disney Legend in 1991

20

July

(1941) At the Hollywood premiere of *The Reluctant Dragon,* Disney's first part–live action, part-animation feature, a riot broke out. It began as a protest by studio animators who, egged on by labor negotiators, had already taken to the picket lines; with all the publicity, the strikers became unruly.

Though it did not recoup its $600,000 costs, *The Reluctant Dragon* has some great moments, such as film of Ward Kimball animating Goofy. That is a clue to the times, since Goofy was primarily the creation of Art Babbitt. Yet Babbitt was on the strike's front lines, and Walt would never forgive him.

DISNEY QUIZ

Who founded the Walt Disney Archives and is author of *Disney A to Z: The Official Encyclopedia?*

Dave Smith

"*I was just not Disney material. I simply could not draw cute little foxes for the life of me.*"

—*Tim Burton, who began his career as a Disney animator*

21
July

(1952) Robin Williams, whose stream-of-consciousness delivery has been a hallmark of much of his work for Disney, was born in Chicago. In his first Disney film, *Good Morning, Vietnam* (1987), Williams famously ad-libbed his monologues and later earned an Oscar nomination. One of his most successful roles featured only his voice: the blue genie of *Aladdin,* created with Williams's vocal talents in mind.

(1924) Another comedic regular in the Disney stable, Don Knotts, was born in West Virginia. His credits include *The Apple Dumpling Gang; Herbie Goes to Monte Carlo;* and *Hot Lead and Cold Feet*—all from the late 1970s.

NAME THAT 'TOON

In what early cartoon do Mickey and Minnie Mouse play a piano duet of "I Can't Give You Anything but Love, Baby" before Mickey launches into "Darktown Strutter's Ball" and eventually "There's No Place Like Home" on the xylophone?

The black-and-white "The Birthday Party" (1931)—and also the color version released a decade later, "Mickey's Birthday Party"

(1994) *The Twilight Zone* Tower of Terror, purportedly housed in the landmark Hollywood Tower Hotel, opened in the Disney-MGM Studios park at Disney World. Looming at the end of Sunset Boulevard, the ride is partly a tribute to Rod Serling's landmark television series and partly a unique thrill-and-chill ride. By the end of 2002, it would be updated four times, and it would become the first attraction ever to be entirely in the computer's control. The most recent version allows the computer to set the drop-and-recover sequence randomly, so that each time guests ride the attraction, they see, feel, and even smell something different.

July

DISNEY QUIZ

What accomplished Hollywood and Broadway dancer served as the dance model for Snow White, giving the animators a guide for the character's movements in the 1937 film?

Marge Champion

23
July

(2002) The soundtrack to the film *The Country Bears* was released, three days before the movie. It was aimed at an older and more musically sophisticated audience than the Country Bear Jamboree park attraction it recalled, and the music received warmer press than the movie. The album featured John Hiatt, Bonnie Raitt, Don Henley, Brian Setzer, Elton John, Bela Fleck, Colin Hay of Men at Work, and the Byrds. Henley, Hiatt, John, Setzer, and Raitt, along with Queen Latifah and Willie Nelson, also appeared in the movie. Bela Fleck's "Bear Mountain Hop" was nominated for a Best Country Instrumental Grammy.

WHERE'S MICKEY?

As early as the 1930s, Mickey was as popular internationally as he was in the States. After "a quick trip around the world," the New York–based correspondent for the *London Daily Herald* wrote, "I have returned to New York to say that Mickey Mouse has been with me most of the way." The Queen of England and Duchess of York were reported to have selected Mickey Mouse china as gifts for 600 children.

24

July

(1985) *The Black Cauldron,* based on the fantasy series The *Chronicles of Prydain,* by Lloyd Alexander, was finally released. A landmark for its struggles, the movie took 12 years to complete, and it cost $25 million—around $10 per drawing. This film was being worked on when Don Bluth and other animators departed and a new generation of artists emerged. *Cauldron* is also a relic of CEO Ron Miller's era, which ended when Roy E. Disney ousted him and returned as animation head. Neither Roy nor new studio head Jeffrey Katzenberg liked it, but there wasn't time to reshape the film or fix the problematic story. It proved a box office disappointment, though many critics admire the animation.

BY THE NUMBERS

Nearly 11 million people—close to twice the original estimate—visited Walt Disney World in its first year. In the first decade, 126 million guests passed through the turnstiles.

Today in

July

(1894) Legendary actor Walter Brennan, who appeared in three live-action Disney films in his 70s, was born in Swampscott, Massachusetts. A former vaudeville performer and three-time Oscar-winning actor, Brennan eventually shifted to TV, where his six years on the popular sitcom *The Real McCoys* introduced him to a whole new generation. His three Disney films—*Those Calloways, The Gnome-Mobile* (in which he played both a gnome and a human millionaire), and *The One and Only, Genuine, Original Family Band*—were all made between 1965 and 1968.

DISNEY QUIZ

In 2004, who was the surprise guest at the ABC Super Soap Weekend at Disney-MGM Studios?

Bob Guiney, a former "Bachelor" and now husband of *All My Children's* Rebecca Budig

(1951) *Alice in Wonderland* had its world premiere in London's Leicester Square Theatre, two weeks before its U.S. release. Although the critics were fairly tolerant, the film was not a hit on either side of the Atlantic, and its failure was another blow to the studios' finances. By some estimates, it lost $2 million, more than canceling out the profits from *Cinderella*. It has gradually become a standard, thanks to fine detail animation; the personality of such characters as the Cheshire Cat (voiced by Sterling Holloway), Mad Hatter (Ed Wynn), and Queen of Hearts (Verna Felton); and the story's sheer familiarity.

26
July

"There was more of Walt in the Carousel of Progress than in anything else we've done."

— *Retired Navy admiral Joseph Fowler, who was charged with building Disneyland, speaking about Walt Disney's involvement in the 1964–65 New York World's Fair*

27
July

(1916) Keenan Wynn, a popular character actor who encouraged his comedian father, Ed Wynn, to go into acting, thus creating a four-generation Hollywood dynasty, was born. Keenan would make a half-dozen films for Disney, including *The Absent-Minded Professor* and *Son of Flubber,* both of which also feature his father; *Snowball Express;* and *The Shaggy D.A.* (The fourth generation of Wynns includes actor-writer Ned Wynn and screen-writer Tracy Keenan Wynn.)

(1962) The Firehouse Five Plus Two, a Dixieland-rag band of Disney animators, designers, and artists led by "Fire Chief" Ward Kimball, recorded a live album at the Golden Horseshoe in Disneyland.

DISNEY QUIZ

Who presented Walt Disney with his special Academy Award for *Snow White and the Seven Dwarfs* in 1939?

Shirley Temple

(1998) The first Disney cruise ship, *Disney Magic,* was christened by Walt Disney's daughter Patty Disney. *Magic* left Port Canaveral on its maiden journey two days later. With a retro Art Deco styling reminiscent of the luxury liners in their heyday, the ship weighs 83,000 tons and has five restaurants, two theaters, and three swimming pools. The *Magic* started with three- and four-day trips to Disney's private island, Castaway Cay, in the Bahamas; beginning in 2001, it began alternating between Grand Cayman, Key West, and Cozumel.

July

LEGENDARY PEOPLE

What pop musician wrote and sang many of the memorable songs for the animated movie *Tarzan,* including the Oscar-winning song "You'll Be in My Heart"?

Phil Collins, named a Disney Legend in 2002

July

(1999) The Rock 'n' Roller Coaster Starring Aerosmith was dedicated by the band—after Steven Tyler and Joe Perry took the ride a dozen times each. It opened to the public the next day and quickly became a must-ride. The story is that riders are headed to an Aerosmith concert in Hollywood, speeding through the S curves of (according to the oversize road signs) Santa Monica Boulevard. Styled like stretch limousines, the attraction's cars go from zero to 60 mph in 2.8 seconds. Written especially for the ride by Tyler and Perry, the soundtrack barrels out of 120 speakers per car.

BY THE NUMBERS

Responding to the September 11 attacks, the touring company of *Aida* and the Los Angeles–based cast of *The Lion King* made a single donation of more than $10,000 to the Red Cross, after turning over all performance receipts from the night of September 12, 2001.

(1907) Roy Williams was born in Coleville, Washington. Williams, known as the "Big Mooseketeer" for his bearlike physique, became the cohost of the original *Mickey Mouse Club* in October 1955. But he had already worked for the Disney Company for a quarter century: as an animator, working on *The Three Caballeros* and *Make Mine Music;* as a cartoon writer; and later as a popular caricaturist at Disneyland.

(1932) Disney released the first full-color "Silly Symphony," "Flowers and Trees," which was transformed from black and white by using the new three-step Technicolor process.

30
July

DISNEY QUIZ

What Disney animator's life-size sculpture of Orville and Wilbur Wright was unveiled in 2002 at the new Wright memorial at Kitty Hawk, North Carolina, commemorating the centenary of their 1903 flight?

Mark Henn

NAME THAT 'TOON

What early Mickey Mouse cartoon was a parody of Buster Keaton's *Steamboat Bill Jr.?*

"Steamboat Willie" (1928)

31
July

(1997) Bob Penfield, who had been employed at Disneyland since a few days before its grand opening in 1955, showed up for his last day at work. He's recognized as the longest-running cast member in the Disney Company. Starting with what he thought was a summer job at Walt Disney's about-to-open park, he would later help out at the 1960 Winter Olympics at Squaw Valley and the 1964–65 World's Fair in New York.

(1995) Disney CEO Michael Eisner announced that the Walt Disney Company would acquire Cap Cities/ABC Entertainment for $19.5 billion, the second-largest commercial merger in U.S. history.

DISNEY QUIZ

What highly regarded California wine label is owned by Ron and Diane Disney Miller?

Silverado Vineyards

August

Jim Henson, creator of the Muppet Show, *poses with some of the characters he personally operated, 1977.*

1

August

(2004) The first annual ESPN: The Weekend fan convention, marking the 25th anniversary of the ESPN network, concluded at the Disney-MGM Studios in Orlando. The event was such a success that the second ESPN weekend was held only seven months later and expanded to three days. The conventions offer fans a chance to mingle with on-camera personalities and athletes, participate in live TV and radio broadcasts, compete in a sports edition of Disney-MGM's game show attraction *Who Wants to Be a Millionaire—Play It!*, and even have their wake-up calls recorded by ESPN personalities.

DISNEY QUIZ

What references to famed fictional detective Sherlock Holmes can be found in the 2003 Disney hit *Shanghai Knights*?

The London villain is named Rathbone, after the quintessential movie *Holmes*, *Basil Rathbone*; the Scotland Yard inspector is named Artie Doyle, as in Sherlock's creator, Arthur Conan Doyle.

August

(2002) *Signs,* the third film for the Disney Company by writer-director M. Night Shyamalan, who had given the studio its most successful live-action film ever, *The Sixth Sense,* was released. Pulling in more than $60 million in its first weekend, more than twice as much as *Sixth Sense* had grossed in its opening weekend, *Signs* became Shyamalan's biggest opening ever. The film eventually earned $200 million. Shyamalan reportedly was approached about writing a fourth Indiana Jones adventure but declined.

DID YOU KNOW?

Sharon Disney remembers watching famed painter Salvador Dalí riding the railroad Walt had built around their house, wearing a full-length coat and cravat despite the summer heat and sitting bolt upright on a little boxcar, his cane planted squarely in front of him.

3

August

(1933) The Ingersoll-Waterbury Clock Co. of Waterbury, Connecticut, released the first Mickey Mouse watch. The timepieces have been in production continuously ever since, although manufactured by various companies. The Ingersoll watch was originally priced at $3.25, though it was eventually lowered to $2.75; a pocket watch sold for $1.50. Ingersoll, which later became Timex, set up a mini watch-making factory at the Century of Progress Exposition in Chicago that drew thousands and made the Mickey Mouse watch the souvenir of choice for fairgoers. By 1935, the company had paid Disney $250,000 in royalties.

NAME THAT 'TOON ——————————

What early film features a cartoon within a cartoon depicting Donald Duck as he receives a 16-mm projector and immediately starts rolling "The Cold-Blooded Penguin," in which Pablo the penguin moves to a tropical island to escape the Antarctic chill but gets homesick?

The Three Caballeros (1945)

4

August

(1901) Louis Armstrong, one of the greats of New Orleans jazz and an influential pop music star, was born in New Orleans. He would perform several times at Disneyland during the 1960s and record an album of songs from Disney films called *Louis Armstrong: Disney Songs the Satchmo Way*. It includes versions of "Zip-a-Dee-Doo-Dah," "When You Wish upon a Star," "The Bare Necessities," and "Whistle While You Work."

BY THE NUMBERS

As the number-one driving attraction in the United States, Walt Disney World welcomed another 100 million guests every three years between 1985 and 1998.

DISNEY QUIZ

What staffer's contributions led to one of the locomotives at Disney World being named in his honor—the only one not named for a Disney family member?

Roger Broggie, head of the studios' machine shop and a major force behind the first railroad at Disneyland

5
August

(1997) "Redux Riding Hood," a quirky sequel to the Grimm fairy tale that takes a somewhat more modern, adult attitude toward the plot, was released. It was nominated for an Academy Award as Best Cartoon Short. Its story line sounds like a spoof of modern angst: the wolf, though prevented from eating Little Red Riding Hood by the woodsman (voiced, funnily enough, by Fabio), manages to survive but comes close to a complete nervous break-down. Eventually he takes the desperate step of constructing a time machine to try to rewrite history, but finds himself caught in the loop.

DID YOU KNOW? ————————————————

According to Cheryl Pecora, head of fireworks entertainment for Walt Disney World and the Disney Cruise Line, a new fireworks display such as Disney World's "Wishes" takes a year to put together, beginning with the concept, then storyboards, and then music; only then is the pyrotechnics designer brought in.

(1999) *The Sixth Sense,* a Hollywood Pictures thriller with two somewhat unlikely stars— Bruce Willis, known first for his comic turns on TV's *Moonlighting* and then for a series of *Die Hard* action films; and a first-time child actor named Haley Joel Osment—was released. In pitching the film, director M. Night Shyamalan described the story as a cross between *The Exorcist* and *Ordinary People. Sixth Sense* would go on to garner four Academy Award nominations and become Disney's most successful non-animated feature ever, earning more than $300 million in the United States and nearly $675 million worldwide.

6

August

LEGENDARY PEOPLE

Though best known as Don Knotts's bumbling partner in *The Apple Dumpling Gang,* what funny man has also been paired with a football-kicking mule (in *Gus*) and a basketball-playing dog (in *Air Bud: Golden Receiver*)?

Tim Conway, named a Disney Legend in 2004

DISNEY QUIZ

Name the three pigs in the Academy Award-winning Disney cartoon "Three Little Pigs" from 1933.

Fiddler Pig, Fifer Pig, and Practical Pig

7

August

(1998) *Snake Eyes,* a Brian De Palma thriller starring Nicolas Cage as a seedy police detective who finds himself caught up in a political assassination conspiracy, was released. The film, which was widely perceived as stylish but shallow, is notable mostly for its cinematic viewpoint: De Palma takes a sort of *Rashomon* approach to the video age, so that several participants—the detective, the naval aide, a mysterious woman, one of the boxers—"see" the same sequence differently (and then there are all the casino's security cameras). De Palma also uses split screens to emphasize simultaneous action.

DID YOU KNOW?

In the waiting area outside the Star Tours attraction at Disneyland and Walt Disney World, visitors hear a page for "Egroeg Sacul," the name of *Star Wars* creator George Lucas spelled backwards.

(1942) *Bambi,* still one of the studios' most popular films, had its world premiere in London. Hobbled by wartime gloom and worldwide distribution cuts, *Bambi,* like *Pinocchio* and *Fantasia,* was not an immediate success. Based on the 1929 novel by Felix Salten, *Bambi* marked an artistic and emotional departure for Disney. The scenes of death are much darker than the fantasy threats and the apparent deaths of Snow White and Sleeping Beauty. But the film gradually captured the American imagination. Rereleased a half-dozen times before coming out on video, it was restored to its original color and released in a special edition again in 2005.

8
August

WHERE'S MICKEY?

Mickey Mouse enjoys great popularity in Japan. Tokyo Disneyland receives more guests than any other theme park in the world.

9

August

(1934) Walt Disney circulated a memo to animators in which he sketched out the characters of the potential dwarfs—not just seven but four dozen of them, some of whom were named Dirty, Cranky, Dizzy, Awful, Blabby, Flabby, and Crabby. The memo described several sequences that ultimately were dropped, including Snow White fleeing through Upside-Downland and a Sleepy Valley full of poppies that may have been inspired by L. Frank Baum's Oz stories. By October 22, the main characters had become more defined. A memo dated that day described Snow White as "a Janet Gaynor type" and Prince Charming as Douglas Fairbanks.

NAME THAT 'TOON

What was Disney's first feature to exclusively use the multiplane camera, which was quite costly but produced a more realistic three-dimensional look?

Pinocchio (1940)

(1959) A story in the *New York Times* announced the plans for the 1964–65 New York World's Fair. Walt Disney, realizing he could use the fair to test his ideas for Disneyland attractions, contacted Robert Moses, the New York City parks commissioner who had been named to head the fair, and offered to collaborate. The Disney Company wound up working on attractions for four pavilions, and the arrangement proved profitable for all. Participating in the World's Fair not only helped finance Disney's designs, particularly the development of audio-animatronics, but formed the basis of Disneyland.

10
August

BY THE NUMBERS

At the height of her fame, Mouseketeer Annette Funicello was reportedly receiving 6,000 pieces of fan mail a day.

DID YOU KNOW?

In Disney World's fireworks show "Wishes," one of the climactic pyrotechnics, the launching of a "wishing star," requires a canister ten inches across and soars 100 feet over Cinderella Castle.

August

(1934) "Orphan's Benefit," which features Mickey Mouse, Donald Duck, and Goofy together, was released—in its original version. In the cartoon, our heroes put on a show to raise money for the kids. Donald makes repeated attempts to recite "Mary Had a Little Lamb," but the mischievous orphans spatter him with eggs until he gives up in disgust. "Orphan's Benefit" was rereleased almost exactly seven years later—a time span that for a while was a Disney tradition—on August 12, 1941, but this time it was in color and contained some additional animation.

LEGENDARY PEOPLE

What early star of the silver screen came out of retirement in 1970 to sing the title song for the animated Disney movie *The Aristocats?*

Maurice Chevalier, named a Disney Legend in 2002

(2005) *The Great Raid,* based on the real-life rescue of more than 500 U.S. prisoners of war from a Japanese camp in the Philippines, was released. It never caught on: its opening-weekend gross was less than $3.4 million, and after three weeks and only $8.5 million worldwide, the movie faded from sight. *The Great Raid* was shot in 2002, but along with several other Miramax and Dimension features, was delayed by the long contract renegotiations between Disney and the Weinsteins, former Miramax heads. When it was agreed that the Weinsteins would leave in September 2005, they pushed to have the films released before then.

12
August

DISNEY QUIZ

What soon-to-be noteworthy cartoonists were among the Disney studio employees who went on strike in 1941?

John Hubley, who would create Mr. Magoo; Bill Hurtz, who would animate *The Rocky and Bullwinkle Show;* Walt Kelly, who would create Pogo and his friends; Bill Melendez, who would turn the popular "Peanuts" comic strips into TV specials; and future "Dennis the Menace" cartoonist Hank Ketcham

13
August

(1932) The studio released "Mickey's Nightmare," in which Mickey falls asleep and dreams that he and Minnie are married, a dream that begins happily but turns more frightening with the arrival of children—Mini Mouses, so to speak. This was the closest to marriage that Mickey and Minnie ever came, at least on camera. In 1933, Walt Disney told a *Film Pictorial* interviewer, "In private life, Mickey is married to Minnie. What it really amounts to is that Minnie is, for screen purposes, his leading lady." But that was the "real" mouse couple; the "stars" simply went steady.

"EPCOT Center is inspired by Walt Disney's creative genius. Here, human achievements are celebrated through imagination, the wonders of enterprise, and concepts of a future that promises new and exciting benefits for all. May EPCOT Center entertain, inform, and inspire. And, above all, may it instill a new sense of belief and pride in man's ability to shape a world that offers hope to people everywhere."

—The dedicatory plaque at Epcot

(1945) Steve Martin, comedian, actor, and onetime Disneyland cast member, was born in Waco, Texas. Martin's family moved to Orange County when he was young, and from age 10 to 18, he worked weekends, after-school hours, and summer vacations in the Main Street Magic Shop at Disneyland. There he perfected not only magic tricks but such vaudeville stunts as balloon-animal sculpture, all bits that he used in appearances on *The Smothers Brothers Show* and *Saturday Night Live*. Since then, Martin has appeared in a number of Disney movies, including the remake of *Father of the Bride,* its sequel, and *Bringing Down the House.*

14
August

BY THE NUMBERS

At Disneyland, the Haunted Mansion is home to 999 ghosts with "room for one more," as the spooky-voiced narrative hints.

DISNEY QUIZ

What was the first Disney attraction to offer two different routes depending on the queue the rider chose, which made guests eager to get in line again?

Mr. Toad's Wild Ride

15
August

(2003) Mission: Space opened at Walt Disney World. It had cost $120 million and involved 650 Imagineers, who logged in 350,000 hours on the project. Putting the concept into action required first-of-its-kind simulators, which combined centrifuge technology and pitch-and-roll motion; and the project relied on years of input from astronaut–turned–Disney consultant Story Musgrave and other NASA advisers as well as scientists from the California Institute of Technology's Jet Propulsion Laboratory. The ride uses centrifugal force, supplied by the same simulators that astronauts use in training, to produce the effect of twice the usual force of gravity. Special effects increase the impression of flight.

DISNEY QUIZ ————————————————

What are the painfully punny names of the two speed slides at Disney World's Typhoon Lagoon?

Stern Burner and Rudder Buster

(1999) *Who Wants To Be a Millionaire?* debuted on ABC. Then hosted by talk show host Regis Philbin, *Millionaire* is a cross between Trivial Pursuit and a pyramid scheme. The game show was originally a summer replacement series, airing nightly for two weeks in August and again in November. In its first year, the show pulled in a record profit of more than $500 million, a rare success for then-beleaguered ABC. Trying to cash in on its popularity, however, ABC began running it four nights a week, and it palled. A syndicated version featuring *The View* cohost Meredith Vieira premiered in 2002.

16
August

NAME THAT 'TOON

What early short features Mickey, Donald, and Goofy as grease monkeys who tear Pete's car apart to find the squeak, discover that it's only a cricket, but then do such a horrendous job trying to piece the car back together that the motor leaps out and chases after Pete?

"Mickey's Service Station" (1935)

17

August

(2005) By this day, the team of the real-life Expedition Everest: Mission Himalayas, a collaboration between Disney Imagineering, Conservation International, and the Discovery Network, had arrived at their destination: the eastern Himalayan mountains. The expedition, expected to last at least two months, was the dream of Imagineering vice president Joe Rohde, creator of the Expedition: Everest attraction at Animal Kingdom. The biologists and botanists from Conservation International and Animal Kingdom went looking for undiscovered species of plants and animals likely to live in the remote conservation sites. Discovery sent teams of cameramen to record the expedition for later airing on the network.

BY THE NUMBERS

One historian has estimated that in sheer footage, Disney's output increased more than fivefold in the war years of 1942–43, 95% of it in government contracts.

DISNEY QUIZ

How does The Many Adventures of Winnie-the-Pooh attraction at Disney World pay tribute to its predecessor, Mr. Toad's Wild Ride?

Near the beginning of the ride, a painted mural depicts Toad handing over the property deed to Owl, and later in the trip a picture shows Mole tipping his hat to Pooh.

18

August

(1956) John Debney, who composed many of Disney's most popular themes, was born. In 1979, when NBC revamped the Disney TV series from *The Wonderful World of Disney* to *Disney's Wonderful World,* Debney composed a new disco-flavored theme for the show. He wrote the score for the "SpectroMagic" parade and music for dozens of Disney movies, including *The Emperor's New Groove, The Princess Diaries,* and *Chicken Little.*

(2004) In a sad coincidence, movie composer Elmer Bernstein died. His hundreds of compositions include one soundtrack for Disney, for the dark (and disappointing) *Black Cauldron* in 1985.

LEGENDARY PEOPLE

During his nearly 40 years of working with the Disney studios, what voice-over artist played the Cheshire Cat in *Alice in Wonderland,* Kaa in *The Jungle Book,* and, most memorably, the beloved Pooh in Disney's *Winnie-the-Pooh* films?

Sterling Holloway, named a Disney Legend in 1991

19
August

(1963) John Stamos, whose acting career has repeatedly intersected with Disney, was born in Cypress, California. Stamos's career began at ABC, though before Disney acquired the network, when he became a romantic hero on *General Hospital*. From 1987 to 1995, he costarred in ABC's *Full House*. In March 2005, Stamos returned to ABC as the star of *Jake in Progress*. A collector of Disney memorabilia, Stamos owns the metal Disneyland banner that stood over the entrance in the 1990s, one of the Dumbo-shaped vehicles from the since-remodeled Flying Elephants ride, and a hellish imp from the defunct Mr. Toad's Wild Ride.

DISNEY QUIZ

What Disney movie icon provided the architectural model for the headquarters of the feature animation department in Burbank?

The building, designed by Robert A. M. Stern and known as the "hat" building, is modeled on the sorcerer's hat from *Fantasia*. (The office occupied by former animation chief Roy E. Disney is cone-shaped.)

BY THE NUMBERS

On Walt Disney's birthday in 1985, the city of Anaheim saluted Disneyland and its creator by releasing one million balloons, a world record.

August

(1960) "The Hound that Thought He Was a Raccoon," a live-action variation on "The Ugly Duckling" with a touch of *The Fox and the Hound,* was released. Based on a story by Rutherford Montgomery called "Weecha the Raccoon," the 48-minute film was intended to be a one-hour television show but was not broadcast until 1964. By then it had been cut nearly in half.

(2005) Filming of *Casanova,* starring Heath Ledger and Jeremy Irons, began in Venice. The script depicts the legendary seducer as having at long last fallen in love, but only because the beautiful Francesca (Sienna Miller) refuses him.

DID YOU KNOW?

The real name of Guy Williams, the star of Disney's 1950s *Zorro* series, was Armand Joseph Catalano. Though his family was Italian, not Spanish, he and the series were so popular in Argentina that he retired there as a celebrity.

21
August

(1920) Christopher Robin Milne, only son of A. A. (Alan Alexander) Milne, was born. He and his stuffed animals inspired one of the most famous friendship stories in children's literature, "Winnie-the-Pooh." Yet the real-life relationship between Christopher Robin and Pooh was rocky. Age 6 when *Winnie-the-Pooh* came out, Christopher grew to resent the attention he got as a famous storybook character and eventually became estranged from his father. While writing his own memoirs after his father's death in 1956, Christopher became reconciled to his past and his father's legacy. He later helped dedicate the Hundred-Aker Wood preserve at A. A. Milne's old farm.

NAME THAT 'TOON

What cartoon marks the last time a Mickey Mouse film was released in black and white while perhaps marking the first time the now-famous boxing kangaroo appeared in the movies?

"Mickey's Kangaroo" (1935)

(1929) "The Skeleton Dance," the first of 75 "Silly Symphony" cartoons, was released. It was largely the brainchild of composer Carl Stalling, and it was animated by Ub Iwerks. Stalling's eerie theme music was a variation not, as is often reported, on Camille Saint-Saëns's "Danse Macabre" but on Edvard Grieg's "March of the Dwarfs," a lucky choice since the studio would soon make its reputation on seven dwarfs. Shortly after the film's release, Stalling followed Iwerks out of the Disney family, apparently thinking that without Iwerks the studio would falter. Stalling moved to Warner Bros., where he oversaw the "Looney Toons" and "Merrie Melodies" cartoons.

August

"Walt Disney World is a tribute to the philosophy and life of Walter Elias Disney and to the talents, the dedication, and the loyalty of the entire Disney organization that made Walt Disney's dream come true. May Walt Disney World bring joy and inspiration and new knowledge to all who come to this happy place, a Magic Kingdom where the young at heart of all ages can laugh and play and learn together."

—Roy O. Disney, at the 1971 dedication of Walt Disney World

23

August

(1986) Marceline, Missouri, the hometown Walt Disney made everyone's hometown, declared August 23 to be Walt Disney Day. On the same day, a resolution began its way through the U.S. Senate to make December 5, which would have been Walt's 85th birthday, a nationwide Walt Disney Recognition Day. The resolution was signed by Disney's old Hollywood friend President Ronald Reagan.

August 23 is now Walt Disney Day throughout the state of Missouri. In 1993, Walt Disney was inducted into the Hall of Famous Missourians, which occupies the third floor of the state capitol rotunda.

DISNEY QUIZ

What is the name of the *Tyrannosaurus rex* skeleton, the largest one ever unearthed, that is being partly excavated at Disney World's Animal Kingdom?

Sue

(1942) *Saludos Amigos* had its world premiere in Rio de Janeiro. The film and its follow-up, *The Three Caballeros,* were inspired by Walt Disney's goodwill trip to South America the year before. He went at the behest of the U.S. government, which, with the advance of World War II, was feeling the pinch of its lost European markets and hoping to encourage trade with its southern neighbors. *Saludos Amigos* (roughly, "Hiya, Friends") links together four animated shorts with live-action footage of Disney and his artists visiting Latin American countries. It was released in the United States in February.

24
August

BY THE NUMBERS

Snow White and the Seven Dwarfs grossed $8.5 million (in 1937 dollars!), making it the highest-grossing film of all time until *Gone with the Wind* hit theaters two years later.

August

(1958) Tim Burton, whose *The Nightmare Before Christmas* has become a holiday tradition at the Haunted Mansion attraction, was born in Burbank, California. One of the first CalArts animation department graduates, Burton joined Disney during the production of *The Fox and the Hound*. He later left but returned to Disney in 1993 to make *Nightmare,* a surprise hit, and a welcome one, for the Touchstone brand. Burton returned to his original inspiration, classic horror movies, for his next Disney film: *Ed Wood* (1994), which won Martin Landau a Best Supporting Actor Oscar for his portrayal of *Dracula* icon Bela Lugosi.

DISNEY QUIZ

What novel inspired the Mr. Toad's Wild Ride attraction at Disneyland?

The Wind in the Willows, by Kenneth Grahame

NAME THAT 'TOON

What cartoon stars Mickey Mouse as a bandleader coaching his group through "The William Tell Overture," while continually being interrupted by an obnoxious peanut vendor, played by Donald Duck, who performs "Turkey in the Straw" on his flute?

"The Band Concert" (1935)

(2005) *The Brothers Grimm,* a fantastic retelling of classic fairy tales, was released. Directed by former Monty Python member Terry Gilliam, it cost $80 million to make and stumbled almost immediately under the weight of poor reviews. If bad things come in threes, *The Brothers Grimm* marked the end of a string of Disney disappointments. Coming two weeks after *The Great Raid,* and one week after *Valiant,* the animated salute to the Royal Air Force in World War II which was critically successful but not popular, this film helped make August 2005 the dog days of Disney.

26
August

"The sanest spot in Hollywood is that studio exclusively devoted to the creation of delicate deliriums and lovely lunacies: the fun factory of Mickey Mouse, Miss Minnie and Mr. Walt Disney, Incorporated."

—*Janet Flanner, in a 1936 article in* **Harper's Bazaar**

27

August

(1964) *Mary Poppins* debuted with an old-fashioned celebrity premiere at Grauman's Chinese Theatre in Hollywood. It went into general release two days later. According to legend, Disney's daughters fell in love with the book and told him the story. He immediately knew the tale was Disney material, but only after years of correspondence and persuasion by Walt and Roy Disney did author P. L. Travers agree to relinquish rights. *Mary Poppins* received 13 Academy Award nominations and won five Oscars, including Best Actress for Julie Andrews, Best Song ("Chim Chim Cher-ee"), and Best Score.

DISNEY QUIZ

What animated resident of Epcot's Journey into Imagination pavilion has, according to his theme song, "Two tiny wings, eyes big and yellow / Horns of a steer, but a lovable fellow? / From head to tail, he's royal purple pigment"?

Figment, a small purple dragon

LEGENDARY PEOPLE

What well-known comedian provided the voice of Scuttle the seagull in the smash hit *The Little Mermaid?*

Buddy Hackett, named a Disney Legend in 2003

28

August

(1957) Two short films, one live-action and one animated, were released; and in many theaters, they were booked together. *Perri*, the only "True-Life Fantasy" (as opposed to the "True-Life Adventures" from which it borrowed its style), was based on a story by Felix Salten and edited from footage shot in Jackson Hole, Wyoming, and the Uinta National Forest in Utah.

The Truth about Mother Goose, also released this day, explains the stories behind three nursery rhymes: "Little Jack Horner," "London Bridge Is Falling Down," and "Mary, Mary, Quite Contrary." Both *Perri* and *Mother Goose* were nominated for the Best Short Film Oscar.

BY THE NUMBERS

In Disney's *20,000 Leagues under the Sea*, the artificial squid—constructed of steel springs, rubber tubing, and Lucite, among other materials—had 40-foot-long tentacles and two 50-foot-long feelers and required 28 handlers.

29

August

(1958) Michael Jackson, onetime child star and longtime King of Pop, was born in Gary, Indiana. In 1985, Jackson approached the Disney Company about a video, just as Disney Imagineers were looking for another project with *Star Wars* creator George Lucas. Lucas and Francis Ford Coppola produced and directed the 3-D "Captain Eo," which showed Jackson dancing in space-age silver. The attraction opened at Epcot in 1986 and ran until 1994; at Disneyland, the film aired from 1986 to 1997. It also had stints in Tokyo and Paris.

NAME THAT 'TOON ————————————————————

In what animated short does a rather rat-faced Mortimer Mouse nearly get both Minnie and Mickey gored by a bull?

"Mickey's Rival" (1936)

(1908) Fred MacMurray, one of the studios' most beloved stars, was born in Chicago. MacMurray was born into the entertainment world and started performing early on. The 1944 thriller *Double Indemnity* marked a turning point for him, and thereafter he made a number of highly regarded films. His career had begun to fade when friend Walt Disney cast him as the Absent-Minded Professor in 1961. The success of that film and its various flubber-ish spin-offs led to MacMurray's long role as Steve Douglas in TV's *My Three Sons*.

30
August

DISNEY QUIZ

What unlikely Animal Kingdom location presents the 3-D *It's Tough To Be a Bug!* show?

The Tree of Life, which has a 425-seat theater inside its trunk

31
August

(1938) Walt and Roy Disney put down a deposit of $10,000, against a final price of $100,000, on a 51-acre site in Burbank near Griffith Park for the new Walt Disney Studios. Disney envisioned a campus with buildings for animators, directors, and ink and paint artists, plus music stages, sound effects studios, and photo lab. They moved in on December 26, 1939. The address, 500 South Buena Vista Street, is now one of the most famous in entertainment. Buena Vista later lent its name to the studios' distribution companies and the official "town" of Walt Disney World near Orlando: Lake Buena Vista, Florida.

DISNEY QUIZ

What Epcot Future World pavilion resembles a pair of glass-sided and slightly askew Egyptian pyramids?

The Journey into Imagination pavilion

September

Actors from the Lion King *musical perform in Dresden, Germany, 2001.*

1

September

(1875) Edgar Rice Burroughs, the creator of one of Disney's most popular figures, was born in Chicago. Though until then he struggled to find his niche, Burroughs struck gold when his very first story, "Tarzan of the Apes," appeared in a pulp magazine in 1912.

After the release of *Snow White and the Seven Dwarfs*, Burroughs himself wrote to Walt Disney suggesting that his ape-man would make an ideal animated star. Though not produced until 1999, *Tarzan* became one of Disney's most successful features, with a worldwide gross of more than $450 million.

DID YOU KNOW? ————————————

Discussing the inspiration for The Indiana Jones Adventure: Temple of the Forbidden Eye thrill ride and *The Indiana Jones Epic Stunt Spectacular,* Imagineer Tony Baxter recalls that the first time he saw the boulder chasing Indiana Jones in *Raiders of the Lost Ark* in 1981, he said, "This would make a fabulous ride."

September

(1979) Big Thunder Mountain opened in Disneyland's Frontierland, followed almost exactly a year later, on September 23, 1980, by a version at Disney World. It has been so popular that a third opened at Tokyo Disneyland in 1987 and another was one of Disneyland Paris's original attractions. It's not surprising that Imagineer Tony Baxter designed so many "mountain" coasters—not only Big Thunder, but Splash Mountain and the Indiana Jones rides—since, like Walt Disney himself, Baxter is a railroad buff. Many of Big Thunder's props are authentic miners' carts, tools, and wheels from Old West ghost towns and scrap shops.

DISNEY QUIZ

What Disney cartoon character turned 50 in 1984 and celebrated with a ticker-tape parade in New York City?

Donald Duck

September

(1910) Yale Gracey, who began as a layout artist and graduated to a special-effects conceptualizer and Imagineer, was born. As one of the lead Imagineers on the Haunted Mansion attraction, he has become the presiding spirit, so to speak, of that theme park ride. Now the Haunted Mansion itself is said to belong to a Master Gracey, and his supposed tombstone lies near the entrance.

(1939) British prime minister Neville Chamberlain interrupted a BBC broadcast of *The Mickey Mouse Show* to announce that Britain and France had declared war on Adolf Hitler and the German nation.

NAME THAT 'TOON —————————

What feature film earned Walt Disney a special technical Oscar award for "outstanding contribution to the advancement of the use of sound in motion pictures" and conductor Leopold Stokowski and his associates a special Oscar for their "creation of a new form of visualized music"?

Fantasia

(1942) "How To Play Baseball," the first of the popular "How To" cartoon series featuring Goofy, was released. In this piece, which set the pattern for the series, Goofy demonstrates by playing all nine positions—for both teams—as well as delivering the various pitches. Over the next couple of years Goofy would play all 22 men in a football game, wind himself into a tangle over golfing diagrams, and hook and nearly strangle himself demonstrating casting and fly-fishing.

4
September

DID YOU KNOW?

The train at Disneyland had its first run before the park's official opening when Walt granted the wish of a young boy suffering from leukemia to ride.

DISNEY QUIZ

In *Pocahontas II: Journey to a New World,* the sequel to *Pocahontas,* who took Mel Gibson's place as the voice of John Smith?

Mel's brother Donal Gibson

5
September

(1930) Pluto made his debut in "The Chain Gang," but, like Goofy, he had no name or identity for a while. Six weeks later, in fact, he appeared in "The Picnic," but as Minnie's pet, then named Rover. Eventually, Minnie's former pet changed allegiance to Mickey, and by May 1931, with the release of "The Moose Hunt," he had a permanent name. In addition to the cartoons in which he costarred with Mickey, Pluto starred in 48 of his own. His voice was created by Pinto Colvig, though Pluto spoke only twice in all those years, including in "The Moose Hunt," where he rowwwrrrs "Kiss me."

LEGENDARY PEOPLE —————————————

What award-winning actress appeared in more than 40 films and starred in a long-running hit TV series, but is best known to children as the teapot in Disney's animated classic *Beauty and the Beast?*

Angela Lansbury, named a Disney Legend in 1995

(1869) Felix Salten, who would inspire *Bambi*, one of Disney's greatest and most emotionally challenging films, was born in Budapest. Unknown to most American audiences, he was an influential figure in 20th-century political literature; his novel *Bambi,* published in 1923, not only was seen as an anti-Nazi parable but also had the distinction of being banned by Hitler's government. Salten lived to see his story made into the Disney film and died on October 8, 1945, five months after the surrender of the Nazi forces and two months after the surrender of Japan.

6
September

BY THE NUMBERS

Totaling more than 8,000 tons, animal manure is the third-largest recycled commodity of the Disney Company. Since 1990, the company has recycled nearly 7,000 tons of material, including plastic, glass, and aluminum.

7

September

(1984) The Morocco pavilion opened in Epcot's World Showcase, the first national pavilion to be added to the original nine. The area was officially opened by Moroccan minister of tourism Mohamed Belmahi. It joined the areas representing Mexico, China, Germany, Italy, Japan, France, the United Kingdom, Canada, and the United States.

DISNEY QUIZ

What *Star Trek* veteran directed Disney's hit movie *Three Men and a Baby?*

Leonard Nimoy

NAME THAT 'TOON

What "Silly Symphony" cartoon focuses on a trio of animals who are abandoned during a snowstorm and take refuge in a house where they proceed to break dishes, "play" the piano, and wreak havoc on their surroundings?

"Three Orphan Kittens" (1935)

8

September

(2000) The long-running ABC series *Boy Meets World*, about an average junior high student who struggles with the usual complications of adolescence and school life, finally concluded its seven-year run. *Boy Meets World* premiered in September 1993, staring Ben Savage as 11-year-old Cory Matthews. As Cory matured during the series, so did the problems, and in the final episode, he flashes back over the previous years as he tries to decide whether to follow Topanga, his longtime—albeit on-again, off-again—girlfriend, to Manhattan. The show ended happily with their marriage.

DID YOU KNOW?

Walt Disney ordered a loudspeaker installed in his office so he could listen to the auditions for the role of Snow White without being influenced by the singers' looks. Adriana Caselotti, who got the part, turned out to be pretty in the Snow White style, with long, dark, wavy hair and large, striking eyes.

9

September

(2005) *An Unfinished Life,* a modern-day Western starring two Oscar winners and an MTV pop diva, premiered. Robert Redford plays a grizzled rancher who has all but let his property, and himself, go to ruin since the death of his only son, a rodeo rider. The one person he is still attached to is his old friend (played by Morgan Freeman), who is slowly recovering from a too-close encounter with a bear. Then the rancher's former daughter-in-law, played by singer Jennifer Lopez, turns up with a face bruised by an abusive boyfriend and with a little girl she says is Redford's granddaughter.

DISNEY QUIZ

Who served as the model for Tarzan's movements through the jungle in Disney's *Tarzan?*

Skateboarder Max Keane, son of Tarzan designer-animator Glen Keane

10

September

(1983) The first Night of Joy festival of contemporary Christian music was held at Disney World's Magic Kingdom. It was so successful that it quickly became an annual event and remains perhaps the most popular contemporary Christian music festival in the country. Since its inception, it is estimated to have drawn nearly a million fans.

On that first occasion, the lineup included Leon Patillo, Shirley Caesar, Petra, and David Meece. The next year the weekend-long festival featured such pop-Christian crossover headliners as Amy Grant and Debby Boone. By 2004 the three "Nights of Joy" hosted two dozen acts and even had special activities for teens.

"I spent a lot of time with Mr. Disney. He took the time to really talk to me and teach me at a very early age about script and character and story arc—things that later in my life would be very, very important to me. . . . He was a great filmmaker, a great man, and a great student of his game."

—Actor Kurt Russell

11
September

(2001) Following news of the terrorist attacks on the World Trade Center towers in New York and the Pentagon in Washington and aboard United flight 93, both Walt Disney World and Disneyland shut down, making this one of the few days in Disney theme park history that the parks on both coasts have been dark. In addition, the Broadway productions of *The Lion King, Beauty and the Beast,* and *Aida,* along with all other New York performances, were canceled.

On September 11, 2002, as part of Broadway's one-year observance of the attacks, Disney's three Broadway shows were once again canceled.

DID YOU KNOW?

For the 2001 movie *Pearl Harbor,* the cost of the reenactment eventually exceeded the cost of the actual attack.

12
September

(2005) Hong Kong Disneyland officially opened. The $3.6 billion project, a joint venture between the Walt Disney Company and the Hong Kong SAR government, includes a theme park closely modeled on Disneyland at Anaheim; two hotels; and retail, dining, and entertainment areas. Disney invested 20% and in return gets 43% of the revenues. The park, only 30 minutes from downtown Hong Kong, was originally forecast to bring in four million visitors in its first year, and ten million by 2010. By its opening, however, estimates were up to 10 million guests every year.

DISNEY QUIZ

When Walt Disney first conceived of Mickey Mouse on that famous train ride home from New York in 1928, what did he want to name him—before Lilly argued against it?

Mortimer

13

September

(1979) Don Bluth, one of the most talented of the younger generation of animators, resigned from the Disney studios to form his own company, eventually taking a dozen other animators with him. It was the third mass defection, after Charles Mintz's luring away of virtually all Walt Disney's animators in 1928 and the union walkout of 1941. The Bluth split, which held up production on *The Fox and the Hound* for several years, marked a serious stylistic divide between the animators of the Nine Old Men's generation and the younger animators of the new era.

NAME THAT 'TOON

What Mickey Mouse cartoon shows Pluto resisting a bath and then, in the resulting fracas, swallowing the soap, which causes him to foam at the mouth and make the townspeople believe he has hydrophobia?

"The Mad Dog" (1932)

(1964) Walt Disney traveled to Washington, D.C., where President Lyndon B. Johnson presented him with the Presidential Medal of Freedom, the highest award given to civilians. It was one of a staggering number of international honors and citations Disney received in his lifetime and after. Former President Dwight D. Eisenhower presented him with the Freedom Foundation Award in 1965. France awarded him the Legion of Honor and the Officer d'Academie ribbons, Thailand its Order of the Crown, Brazil its Order of the Southern Cross, and Mexico the Order of the Aztec Eagle. He was posthumously awarded a Congressional Gold Medal in 1968.

14
September

DISNEY QUIZ

In *Dragonslayer,* what is the name of the dragon, which represents Disney's main contribution to this Paramount production?

Vermithrax Pejorative

15
September

(1999) The approach of Hurricane Floyd forced the closure of Walt Disney World, marking the first time any Disney park had not opened for business on time. Floyd was not only a powerful Category 3 hurricane, but also nearly twice the size of the typical Atlantic Ocean hurricane, measuring almost 600 miles across. The night before its expected strike, park officials told only essential employees to come into work. Floyd made landfall at Cape Fear, North Carolina, about 3 a.m. on September 16, and the worst of the storm had bypassed Disney World. Animal Kingdom opened at noon, and the other parks reopened the next morning.

LEGENDARY PEOPLE

What TV star served as the main host for the live broadcast of Disneyland's opening in 1955—and, as pay for the job, was given exclusive rights to the park's camera and film concessions for the next ten years?

Art Linkletter, named a Disney Legend in 2005

16

September

(1963) Composer and conductor Oliver Wallace, whose Disney scores included *Dumbo* (which won him an Oscar), *Alice in Wonderland, Peter Pan,* and *Cinderella,* died in Los Angeles. Born in London in 1887, Wallace began as a pianist ad-libbing accompaniment to silent films. He came to work for Disney in 1936. Animator Frank Thomas later described him as "a madman, funny, eccentric, noisy, unexpected, and loved by everyone. . . . He was primarily an improvising musician, with a great sense of music; and from his years of playing piano to silent movies he was able to match music to any piece of action."

DID YOU KNOW?

Fess Parker, who played Davy Crockett in the Disney TV series, not only could not ride horses but was allergic to them—and to Davy's leather breeches, which gave him rashes.

DISNEY QUIZ

For whom are Hugo and Victor, two of the supportive gargoyles in *The Hunchback of Notre Dame,* named?

Victor Hugo, the author of the novel on which the film is based

17

September

(1991) *Home Improvement,* starring Tim Allen as the not-so-handy host of a handyman series on television, debuted on ABC. This was the first, but far from the last, Disney appearance for Allen, who became a familiar Disney face and voice and even went on to release a best-seller called *Don't Stand Too Close to a Naked Man* via Disney's Hyperion Books. Allen provided the voice of Buzz Lightyear for both *Toy Story* and *Toy Story 2,* and for cartoon series afterward. He also starred as the new Santa in *The Santa Clause.*

DISNEY QUIZ

In what Disney movie did the lighthouse, constructed on a set in Burbank and set up near Morro Bay, California, look so authentic that Disney execs had to get clearance from the Coast Guard to operate it, so that real ships wouldn't be misled?

Pete's Dragon

DID YOU KNOW?

While playing President Franklin D. Roosevelt in the movie *Pearl Harbor* (2001), actor Jon Voight wore steel braces on his legs that were identical to the president's own. As a result, Voight suffered continual chafing and bruising, another secret FDR had kept from the public.

18

September

(1928) Walt Disney's application for trademark protection on the character of Mickey Mouse was granted by the U.S. copyright office. Disney filed the application as he and Ub Iwerks were secretly putting together *Plane Crazy,* which was to have been Mickey's debut film. After Walt's earlier discovery that he did not own the rights to Oswald the Lucky Rabbit, he swore never to make that mistake again.

Disney's first legal suit, filed against a version of *Aesop's Fables* featuring a suspiciously familiar rodent, was successful. Walt was granted a second trademark, for the use of the Mickey image in motion pictures, the next year.

WHERE'S MICKEY?

Marty Sklar, vice-chairman and principal creative executive of Walt Disney Imagineering, sports a brass Mickey Mouse ring and wears a three-dial Mickey Mouse watch set to the times in Los Angeles, Paris, and Tokyo to keep track of the theme parks.

19
September

(1959) Nikita Khrushchev, premier of what was then the Union of Soviet Socialist Republics, the military and political rival of the United States, was in this country to meet with President Dwight D. Eisenhower and demanded to visit Disneyland. He was turned down. The diminutive and willful Khrushchev, whose childish temper tantrums he had intentionally made famous, wanted to join his wife and daughter at Disneyland. However, because of security concerns expressed by the Los Angeles police chief, he was not allowed to go. Instead, while his family enjoyed the rides, he was fobbed off on a luncheon of Hollywood executives.

BY THE NUMBERS

Stormalong Bay, the swimming area at the Beach Club Resort at Walt Disney World in Orlando, holds 750,000 gallons of water, making it the largest sand-bottom pool in the world.

DISNEY QUIZ

What animated trio serves as Jessica Rabbit's backup musicians in *Who Framed Roger Rabbit?*

The three crows from *Dumbo*

(2003) Two of the company's most popular modern children's series, *Lizzie McGuire* and *That's So Raven,* transferred from the Disney Channel to ABC as part of the revamped Saturday-morning lineup. *Lizzie McGuire,* a part–live action, part-animated series about the trials and tribulations of a 13-year-old girl, premiered on the Disney Channel in January 2001 with Hilary Duff in the title role.

That's So Raven was a vehicle for Raven, veteran of *The Cosby Show* and *Hangin' with Mr. Cooper.* It first debuted in Britain in September 2002, shifted to the Disney Channel in January 2003, and then moved to ABC.

20
September

WHERE'S MICKEY?

Walt Disney World in Orlando displays bronze statues both of Walt Disney with Mickey Mouse and of Roy Disney with Minnie Mouse, but only Walt and Mickey are at Disneyland; the copy of the Roy and Minnie statue was installed at the Disney studios in Burbank instead. Both statues were done by Disney master sculptor Blaine Gibson.

21

September

(2001) Marceline, Missouri, which Walt Disney called home for five years, celebrated the centennial of his birth with a three-day commemoration. Most of the activities took place along Marceline's Main Street, inspiration for the Main Street, USA, at the heart of the Magic Kingdom.

Also on this date, a report confirmed that the Bass brothers of Texas had sold more than 1.35 million shares of Disney stock on margin, bringing them $2 billion in cash. The transaction was an embarrassment for then-CEO Michael Eisner, who considered them close allies. For years, Sid Bass, Roy Disney, Stanley Gold, and Eisner had exercised nearly total control over the board of directors. Bass's departure would eventually prove costly to Eisner's cause.

DID YOU KNOW?

Disney archivist Dave Smith debunks a widespread rumor about the movie *Three Men and a Baby*. A "ghostly" figure glimpsed in the background was suspected to be the spectre of a child who had lived in the house where the movie was filmed, but Smith says that the ghost was a forgotten prop and that there was no house, just a set on a Toronto soundstage.

(1936) In one of the most famous behind-the-scenes performances ever, Walt Disney regaled animators and directors with a nearly shot-by-shot, line-by-line description of *Snow White and the Seven Dwarfs*. The meeting lasted more than three hours. Walt's one-man performance represented the most astonishing example of his obsession with this movie's details. In a similar meeting a few months earlier, he spent considerable time discussing just how the sequence with the huntsman, the bird, and Snow White should be framed to dramatize the huntsman's change of heart.

22

September

NAME THAT 'TOON

What animated short earned Walt Disney his first scientific and technical Oscar for the development of the multiplane camera?

"The Old Mill" (1937)

"Laughter is America's most important export."

—*Walt Disney*

23
September

(2005) The Walt Disney World Triathlon weekend began with a sports merchandising expo and a kids' triathlon. This was only one in a series of such events. Two weeks later, on October 8, the Wide World of Sports complex hosted a similar "go the distance" expo and the Susan G. Komen Central Florida Race for the Cure, a 5K walk-run that funds breast cancer research. The next day, the "Race for the Taste" 10K promoted the annual Epcot Food and Wine Festival, with runners beginning the race at Disney-MGM Studios with a toast and hors d'oeuvres and running around the Boardwalk before winding up at Epcot.

DISNEY QUIZ ————————————————————

In *Who Framed Roger Rabbit,* Kathleen Turner famously provided Jessica Rabbit's sultry speaking voice, but who supplied the character's singing voice?

Amy Irving, coproducer Steven Spielberg's then-wife

(1984) Michael Eisner walked into the Burbank offices as the new chairman and CEO of the Walt Disney Company. He had been elected two days earlier, following the ouster of Ron Miller, Walt's son-in-law. When he took over, Walt Disney Productions was more than $900 million in debt; within three years the company was $340 million in the black. Though he would eventually lose his title as chairman of the board and retire early, Eisner was long viewed not merely as the second coming of Walt Disney but as one of the world's top entertainment moguls, with a fool-proof sense of the public appetite.

24
September

DID YOU KNOW?

On September 11, 1968, the U.S. Postal Service unveiled a six-cent stamp featuring a portrait of Walt Disney. Another and larger set of stamps, a series of four each, was commissioned in 2003.

25

September

(2001) A sitcom set in a hospital debuted; exactly one year later, so did another. Only one survived. *Scrubs,* a Touchstone Television (for NBC) series that premiered in 2001, focuses on doctor J. D. (Zach Braff) and his fellow first-year interns at a teaching hospital. It has a small cult following based on its many guest stars, thanks to appearances by Dick Van Dyke, Michael J. Fox, and more. *MDs,* which premiered in 2002, was a rehash of the *M*A*S*H* formula, only with the modern HMO and mega-insurance establishment as the villain. *MDs* died a quick death; ABC execs pulled the plug in December.

DISNEY QUIZ ————————————

What film, its songs, and a few of its characters served as inspiration for the Splash Mountain attraction, which opened first at Disneyland in Anaheim in 1989?

Song of the South

26
September

(1953) Walt Disney summoned a former employee, artist Herb Ryman, to help him create a conceptual drawing of Disneyland that Roy Disney could show to prospective backers. Two days later, when they emerged, Ryman had completed an elaborate sketch based on Walt's descriptions. Armed with the drawing and a detailed description of the park, Roy flew to New York to pitch an hour-long television program. The marathon design session was dubbed "the lost weekend." ABC eventually made an offer: Disney would supply ABC with a TV series, and the network would invest $500,000 in the park and guarantee another $4.5 million in loans.

LEGENDARY PEOPLE

Under contract with Disney studios, what actor headlined in some of Disney's box-office greats, including *The Love Bug, That Darn Cat,* and *The Shaggy D.A.?*

Dean Jones, named a Disney Legend in 1995

27
September

(1947) The part–live action, part-animation *Fun and Fancy Free* was released, marking the first time that Walt Disney himself had not supplied Mickey Mouse's voice. *Fun and Fancy Free* was a story within a story, or maybe three. The most popular section, which was often run on Disney's television shows, was "Mickey and the Beanstalk." While the cartoon was being filmed, Walt Disney was tied up with other business, so Jim Macdonald provided the familiar mouse's squeak. "Fill-in" Macdonald continued to supply the voice of the world's most famous mouse for 30 years.

DISNEY QUIZ ——————————————

What Disney film features Oscar winner Hattie McDaniel, who had won a Best Supporting Actress award in 1939 for her performance as Scarlett O'Hara's moral-minded Mammy in *Gone with the Wind?*

Song of the South

"Of all of our inventions for mass communication, pictures still speak the most universally understood language."

—*Walt Disney*

(1964) *Greyfriars Bobby,* which had originally been released as a theatrical film, had its first television airing on *Walt Disney's Wonderful World of Color.* Now a sentimental favorite, it had not performed as well as expected when first released because many Americans reportedly found the authentic Scots' accents difficult to understand.

The film, from a book by Eleanor Atkinson, is based on a true story from 19th-century Edinburgh about an aging shepherd and his Skye terrier Bobby, who remains devoted to his owner even after the man's death. Eventually, the dog is granted official "freedom of the city" for his loyalty.

28
September

NAME THAT 'TOON

What recent Disney-Pixar film showcases Paul Newman as the voice of a 1951 Hudson Hornet called Doc and also features such race-car drivers as Richard Petty?

Cars (2006)

29
September

(2005) *The Night Stalker,* an updated supernatural mystery show based on a 1970s TV series, premiered on ABC. The original *Night Stalker* (1972) was the most watched TV movie of its time; it inspired first a sequel, *The Night Strangler* (1973), and then a 1974 series called *Kolchak: The Night Stalker,* all starring Darren McGavin. *X-Files* creator Chris Carter has said the old show was one of his inspirations, and the 21st-century *Night Stalker* creator Frank Spotnitz and producer-director Dan Sackheim, both of whom are *X-Files* veterans, were apparently repaying the compliment.

DID YOU KNOW? ————————————————

On December 5, 1986, which would have been Walt Disney's 80th birthday, the U.S. government declared an official Walt Disney Recognition Day.

(2005) Harvey and Bob Weinstein, who founded Miramax Film Corp. in 1979 and sold it to the Disney Company in 1993, departed the Disney fold. The settlement was estimated at $130 million, which included their 2004 and 2005 bonuses, although that figure did not include the cost of buying back some 40 projects from the Disney Company. The Weinsteins left behind the Miramax name, its 55-film catalog, and the book-publishing division, although they retained the Dimension Films label. The brothers said they intended to create a "fully integrated media company" dealing in movies, TV, the Internet, books, and theater.

30
September

DISNEY QUIZ

What is the only film in which both Mickey Mouse and Bugs Bunny appear?

Who Framed Roger Rabbit (1988)

October

Julie Andrews dances with chimney sweeps during the filming of Mary Poppins, *1963.*

(1971) Walt Disney World in Orlando celebrated the grand opening of the Magic Kingdom. The expected crowds stayed away— fearing crowds. Only about 10,000 guests came to the Magic Kingdom on its first day. But by the holiday season, attendance had boomed.

1
October

Exactly 11 years later, on October 1, 1982, Epcot, then known as EPCOT Center, opened with five Future World and nine World Showcase pavilions complete. Now, October 1 marks a double anniversary for the Orlando theme park.

WHERE'S MICKEY?

In George Lucas's first film, the grim *THX 1138,* one of the baby Ewoks clutches a stuffed Mickey Mouse toy, and one of the robots wears a Mickey watch.

NAME THAT 'TOON

In what cartoon does Goofy play a sort of Jekyll and Hyde of the highway: calm Mr. Walker, the pedestrian, and maniacal Mr. Wheeler, the demonic driver?

"Motor Mania" (1950)

October

(2004) A suburban black comedy, *Desperate Housewives,* debuted on ABC to an astonishing first-time audience of 21.3 million Americans. Suddenly the show, the title phrase, and the fictional Wisteria Lane, Fairview, were national obsessions, sparking fan blogs and fashion trends. It was a welcome surprise for ABC, which had not had a major hit since *Who Wants To Be a Millionaire?* in 2002. Within months, the price for a 30-second commercial slot during *Desperate Housewives* nearly tripled, from $125,000 to $350,000.

In 2005, Teri Hatcher, Felicity Huffman, and Marcia Cross were nominated for the Emmy Award for Outstanding Lead Actress in a Comedy. Huffman won that award, while Hatcher won the 2005 Golden Globe for Best Performance by an Actress in a Television Series—Musical or Comedy.

"Throughout the centuries there were men who took first steps down new roads armed with nothing but their own vision."

—Ayn Rand, **The Fountainhead,**
quoted on a wall of the American Adventure at Epcot

(1955) The original *Mickey Mouse Club* debuted on ABC, with hosts Jimmie Dodd and Roy Williams and its first 24 Mouseketeers. Over the next two seasons, another 15 Mouseketeers joined the cast. The show began with the famous theme song "The Mickey Mouse Club March," written by Dodd. Every day had its own theme, from "Fun with Music" Mondays to "Talent Roundup" on Fridays. A total of 260 one-hour shows and 130 half-hour shows aired before the series ended in September 1958; they reran from 1962 to 1965 and again in 1975.

3
October

DISNEY QUIZ

Before settling on the name Roy, what did Walt Disney's father, Elias, want to name his third son?

Columbus, to pay tribute to the World Columbian Exposition, which had given Elias many commissions for furniture and designs

4
October

(2004) The flagship World of Disney Store on Manhattan's Fifth Avenue had its grand opening, complete with Cinderella and Prince Charming riding down Fifth Avenue in their horse-drawn crystal carriage, announced by royal trumpeters. The three-story, 24,000-square-foot store opened to the public the next day.

This was actually a reopening, since this store had begun in 1996 as the flagship Disney Store. But after that chain expanded to more than 700 branches, sales fell and the stores were sold or closed. The World of Disney Stores, including a huge one in Orlando's Downtown Disney Marketplace, are a new, more limited chain concept.

DID YOU KNOW? ——————

In the original "Three Little Pigs" (1933), the wolf comes to the pigs' home disguised as a Jewish peddler, a crude racist stereotype that was edited out a few years later.

5

October

(1949) The double cartoon feature *The Adventures of Ichabod and Mr. Toad,* showcasing Bing Crosby and Basil Rathbone as celebrity storytellers, was released. The featurette that retells Washington Irving's *The Legend of Sleepy Hollow* may be better known, but the Toad story, based on Kenneth Grahame's *The Wind in the Willows,* inspired the popular Disneyland attraction Mr. Toad's Wild Ride and an even more elaborate pavilion (since closed) at Walt Disney World.

This double feature would turn out to be the last of the package releases. As the studios' finances began to improve, Walt Disney would return to making full-length features.

BY THE NUMBERS

Not that the Disney Company wants to suggest that Americans are getting heftier, but the water-filled crash-test dummies used for the Grizzly River Run attraction at Disney's California Adventure weighed 200 pounds apiece.

6

October

(1927) Warner Bros.' groundbreaking film *The Jazz Singer*, with Al Jolson, premiered in New York City, where the young Walt Disney saw it. It convinced Disney, who had just completed the first two Mickey Mouse cartoons and was in New York trying to sell them to a distributor, that sound would be an integral element of all films in the future. He immediately declared that the next cartoon—the one that would become "Steamboat Willie" (1928)—would have a soundtrack that included music, and that the two completed cartoons would be remade with sound.

DISNEY QUIZ

What two French romantic painters inspired the look of Disney's *Beauty and the Beast?*

Fragonard and Boucher

LEGENDARY PEOPLE

What eight-time Oscar-winning composer contributed catchy songs to hits such as *The Little Mermaid, Aladdin,* and *Pocahontas?*

Alan Menken, named a Disney Legend in 2001

October

(1971) The part–live action, part-animation *Bedknobs and Broomsticks* was released in London. It was released in the United States in December. The movie not only resembled the similarly mixed-format *Mary Poppins,* it had much of the same crew behind it, including director Robert Stevenson and producer-writer Bill Walsh, who elaborated on the stories written by Mary Norton (also author of the popular children's books about the Borrowers). Though the film was not as successful as Disney had hoped, it won an Oscar for Best Special Effects and has evolved into a fairly popular standard.

DID YOU KNOW?

A story in the December 1940 *Atlantic Monthly* describes the Disney studios' library as containing "a battery of steel filing cabinets which hold a million and a half typed and classified jokes, each legally ascribed to the source from which it was set down. There are 124 classifications of such jokes, and each has from five to twenty subclassifications. . . . Along one wall is a steel file of sixteen solid cabinets of cartoon jokes, labeled 'Inventions, Mountains, Costume, Mummies, Tunnels, Panthers, Astronomy, Liar, Household, Moderne, Local, Military, Party, Climate, Crime, Organizations, People, Radio, Real Estate, Scandal, Sciences, Sports, Fish Holidays, Art, Birth, Anatomy, Appearances, Baby Ailments, and Dumb Dames.' "

8

October

(1996) The spa at Disney World's Grand Floridian Hotel opened to the public. It was considered so much a draw in the increasingly body-conscious 1990s that the phrase "and Spa" was added to the eight-year-old resort's name. Following on the heels of the new spa at the Disney Institute, this hotel addition was part of the company's campaign to capture not only an adult audience but also a more upscale clientele. The Grand Floridian's spa, located in a separate pavilion that insulates guests from the hotel bustle, offers a wide range of body wraps, herbal scrubs, hydromassage, reflexology, and thassalotherapy.

NAME THAT 'TOON —————————————————

For what feature did Disney animators study Louis Prima's Las Vegas act as inspiration for his character, an orangutan?

The Jungle Book

"Disneyland celebrated its 40th anniversary by burying a time capsule. They say it will be dug up in 50 years—or when the last person in line at Space Mountain gets to the front, whichever comes first."

—Jay Leno

9

October

(2003) "Wishes," one of the largest fireworks shows ever created, debuted at the Magic Kingdom at Walt Disney World. Not only is it several times more expensive than its predecessor, "Fantasy in the Sky," but it runs five minutes longer and requires almost 700 shells, fired by 533 all-computerized cues. Fireworks designer Eric Tucker uses layering techniques, which means that some effects are fired from closer proximity to the audience. Conceived as a storytelling performance, "Wishes" links parts of 15 songs involving wishes, such as "When You Wish upon a Star" and "A Dream Is a Wish Your Heart Makes."

DISNEY QUIZ

What voice-over artist coinvented the Heimlich antichoking maneuver, though Henry Heimlich got the name recognition?

Paul Winchell, voice of Tigger in Disney's Winnie-the-Pooh films

10

October

(**1957**) *Zorro,* one of the studios' most popular series, debuted on ABC. Altogether, a total of 78 episodes aired over two years, plus two hour-long versions. Although the series was still popular, ABC declined to buy it for a third year, calculating that they could make more money producing their own shows in-house. When ABC tried to prevent Disney from offering either *Zorro* or *The Mickey Mouse Club* to another network, Walt and Roy Disney bought out ABC's share. The shows were later colorized for airing on the Disney Channel.

DID YOU KNOW? ————————

In 2001, the National Building Museum board presented the Disney Company and Eisner with its annual award for quality architecture. Robert A. M. Stern, Michael Graves, Frank Gehry, and Aldo Rossi—all of whom worked on EuroDisney and other Disney projects—were among the architects specifically mentioned in the award.

(2003) The ExtraTERRORestrial Alien Encounter at Walt Disney World's Tomorrowland ceased operation. A collaboration between *Star Wars* creator George Lucas and Disney Imagineers, Alien Encounter originally opened in June 1995, though only after Michael Eisner insisted a few more chills be added to the thrills. With creepy special effects involving air jets and vibrators, it played to the audiences of movies such as the *Alien* series.

After Alien Encounter closed, the attraction was recast as the barely scary Stitch's Great Escape! and reopened a year later.

11
October

DISNEY QUIZ

What animated character is an almost mythological composite of a lion's mane, a buffalo's skull frame and beard, a wild boar's tusks and muzzle, a gorilla's forehead, a bear's torso, and the legs and tail of a wolf?

The Beast in *Beauty and the Beast*

12
October

(1994) Former Walt Disney Studios chairman Jeffrey Katzenberg (who resigned when CEO Michael Eisner declined to name him company president), film producer-director Steven Spielberg, and record-company executive David Geffen announced their new movie studio, ultimately called Dreamworks SKG. Although its success has been uneven, it had huge hits with *Shrek,* which was filled with none-too-flattering Disney references, and *Antz,* which Disney and Pixar execs charged was a lift from *A Bug's Life.*

In 1996, Katzenberg filed suit against Disney claiming he was due $12.5 billion for the projects he had initiated while there. After three years of litigation, Katzenberg got his settlement: $280 million.

NAME THAT 'TOON ————————————

What early Mickey Mouse short represents Disney's tribute to Charles Lindbergh?

"Plane Crazy," (1928)

13

October

(1940) Dave Smith, founder of the Walt Disney Archives, was born in Pasadena, California. While working at UCLA's Research Library, Smith compiled a bibliography of Disney-related materials in the stacks. In June 1970, the Walt Disney Archives were established, with Smith as archivist. Smith and his staff, which has grown to nine, collect and preserve materials relating to Disney history, provide research assistance to Disney employees, and answer inquiries from journalists, writers, and Disney fans. Under Smith's watch, the archives have become the arbiter of information on movie releases, casting news, park amusements, cruise itineraries, hirings and firings, Oscars, Emmys, Legends, and more.

DID YOU KNOW?

When Imagineers were trying to talk CEO Michael Eisner into the idea for Animal Kingdom, senior creative executive Joe Rohde allegedly led a leashed tiger into a meeting to prove that people find wild animals fascinating. Eisner concurred, and planning proceeded.

14

October

(1926) The first Winnie-the-Pooh book, by A. A. Milne, was published in the United Kingdom. The original sales of 20 million copies in the United Kingdom were far exceeded by U.S. and foreign-language sales. Pooh would later become a symbol of Walt Disney Productions as identifiable, and a merchandising image as successful, as Mickey Mouse.

The Pooh stories were inspired by the author's son, Christopher Robin, who had a stuffed bear named Edward and later befriended a bear at the London Zoo named Winnipeg. Edward, so the story goes, tells Christopher Robin that he wants a more impressive name, which gets borrowed from a swan at the zoo called Pooh.

DISNEY QUIZ

What British political cartoonist was brought in to consult on the character design in the Disney film *Hercules*, mainly influencing the figure of Hades?

Gerald Scarfe

(1971) Two weeks after Walt Disney World's grand opening, *Life* magazine hit newsstands with a cover photo of 1,500 Disney employees in front of Cinderella Castle. The shoot took place two months earlier. Even though park construction was running behind, with publicity in mind, Disney executives called up the entire cast—musicians, mimes, vendors, street sweepers, cooks, Mickey, Minnie, Snow White, and the dwarfs—all in full costume. Although it took most of this hot August day for photographer Yale Joel to set up spotlighting and reflectors and to take light readings and test shots, he clicked the shutter just once before proclaiming the shot perfect.

15
October

LEGENDARY PEOPLE

Who made coonskin caps stylish when he wore one as American historical character Davy Crockett in a three-part Disney television show in the 1950s?

Fess Parker, named a Disney Legend in 1991

16
October

(1923) Walt and Roy Disney formalized their partnership, incorporating as the Disney Brothers Cartoon Studio, so that they could sign a contract with Margaret Winkler to distribute their first series, the half-animated "Alice" shorts.

The second order of business that day was to sign up Alice. The series' pilot, "Alice's Wonderland," had been made in Kansas City with six-year-old Virginia Davis as Alice. Since Winkler had made the deal contingent on Virginia, Walt wrote to the Davises urging them to move to Hollywood for the project, but they were reluctant. Roy Disney's fiancée, Edna Francis, talked with Virginia's parents and sealed the deal.

DISNEY QUIZ

What future Miss America debuted in 1992 as Ariel in the live Voyage of the Little Mermaid attraction at Walt Disney World?

Leanza Cornett, Miss America 1993

"I would rather entertain and hope that people learned something than educate people and hope they were entertained."

—*Walt Disney*

17

October

(1925) Jack Wagner, one of the most familiar but most anonymous Disney cast members, was born. For 20 years, beginning in 1970, Wagner was known as the Voice of Disneyland. He recorded most of the park announcements and directions, starting with "Hello, and welcome to the Magic Kingdom." Wagner gives the caution speech at Space Mountain and is the "Old Man" at Big Thunder Mountain. He also recorded scripts for Disney World, Tokyo Disneyland, and Disneyland Paris. Yet Wagner's most famous words must be "Please stand clear of the doors; *Por favor, mantengan se alejado de las puertas*"—the trademark of the monorail.

DID YOU KNOW?

Walt's parents, Flora and Elias, were so close to their pastor, Walter Parr, that they named their child for him. The admiration was mutual, and when the pastor's own son was born the day after Walt, he named him Elias.

18

October

(1967) *The Jungle Book* opened in general release. It was the last animated feature that Walt Disney himself supervised (although it was released nearly a year after his death). It was also one of the studios' biggest box office hits, earning more than $200 million worldwide, and the first of several overlapping adaptations of the Kipling stories the Disney studios produced. Part of this movie's success came from the unusually expressive actors—including Phil Harris, Sebastian Cabot, Louis Prima, and Sterling Holloway—whose audible personalities influenced the animals' animation. Terry Gilkyson's "The Bare Necessities" was nominated for an Oscar.

DISNEY QUIZ

Because Jim Jordan, the voice of Orville the albatross in *The Rescuers*, had passed away before making the sequel, Orville's brother was introduced in *The Rescuers Down Under*. What was he "Wright-ly" named?

Wilbur

(1996) The first ABC Super Soap Weekend was held at Disney-MGM Studios at Disney World. By 2000, the theme park was reporting capacity crowds for the event. In 2003, more than 30 ABC stars came to meet and greet fans, who also enjoyed celebrity motorcades, talk shows, and soap-opera trivia versions of *Who Wants to Be a Millionaire*—Play It! As owner of ABC, Disney invites only actors from ABC dramas: now *All My Children, One Life to Live,* and *General Hospital.* But the lineup for the weekend, now held in mid-November, always includes some heavy hitters, such as Susan Lucci and Kelly Monaco.

19
October

WHERE'S MICKEY? ——————

Famed architect Michael Graves designed the Mickey Mouse teapot, complete with little shoes and gloves, and a whole line of kitchen implements and accessories.

20

October

(1983) "Mickey's Christmas Carol," the mouse's first theatrical cartoon appearance in 30 years, premiered in England. It was released in the United States on December 16 and was nominated for the Best Short Film Oscar. The film not only marked Mickey's return to the big screen but also introduced a new Mickey, voice-over artist Wayne Allwine. (The last time Mickey had been featured, in 1953, Jim Macdonald had done the talking.)

Someone new was now drawing Mickey as well: Mark Henn, whose creations include *Little Mermaid* Ariel and young Simba of *The Lion King.*

DID YOU KNOW?

Disney's live-action *The Story of Robin Hood and His Merrie Men* (1952), which most critics like better than the more popular animated *Robin Hood* of 1973, was made in England because Walt Disney had money there he could not retrieve.

(2003) Walt Disney World hosted a railway celebration in honor of Walt Disney's fascination with trains. The event also served as a reminder that the original Disneyland park was partly inspired by Walt's hobby. It was not simply that Walt was a train buff; trains became a major element in his conception of an amusement park. As early as 1948, he wrote a memo describing his idea for a park that featured a railroad station and was circumnavigated by the tracks. A railway is also a major feature of Disney World's Magic Kingdom, and miniature trains run through Epcot's World Showcase.

21
October

DISNEY QUIZ

What Hollywood actress wore a pirate's costume to the premiere of Disney's *Pirates of the Caribbean?*

Daryl Hannah

NAME THAT 'TOON

Starring Donald Duck as the owner of a miniature train that he has built in his backyard, what short is a mild joke about the trouble Walt put his engineers and technicians through when he constructed the Carolwood-Pacific Railroad at his own home?

"Out of Scale" (1951)

22

October

(1997) The *Orlando Sentinel* published a story saying Walt Disney World officials planned to close the Mr. Toad's Wild Ride attraction and replace it with one based on Winnie-the-Pooh. Upon reading the article, Toad fan John LeFante organized an Internet letter-writing campaign (www.savetoad.com) and proposed a live protest at the resort. A *Miami Herald* story launched a similar protest, and the first of four "Toad-Ins" was held on December 7, 1997. But in September 1998, the attraction closed, and The Many Adventures of Winnie-the-Pooh opened in June 1999. At Disneyland, versions of both rides peacefully coexist.

"Somehow I can't believe that there are any heights that can't be scaled by a man who knows the secrets of making dreams come true. This special secret, it seems to me, can be summarized in four C's. They are Curiosity, Confidence, Courage, and Constancy, and the greatest of all is Confidence. When you believe in a thing, believe in it all the way, implicitly and unquestionably."

—Walt Disney

23

October

(1941) *Dumbo* premiered in New York City. Unlike the previous films *Fantasia* and *Pinocchio, Dumbo* was a bargain, made for a little more than $800,000 and bringing a profit of $850,000. The film won a Best Score Oscar for Frank Churchill and Oliver Wallace, and the lullaby "Baby Mine" was nominated for Best Song.

(1959) The first episode of *The Swamp Fox,* one of Disney's most popular series, premiered, with Leslie Nielsen as South Carolina's Revolutionary War guerilla hero Francis Marion.

DID YOU KNOW?

Some historians have calculated that *Tarzan of the Apes* had been made into live-action movies **46** times before the Disney studios set out to create the animated version in the 1990s. (Only *Dracula* has been filmed more often.)

24

October

(1947) Walt Disney testified, along with long-time friend and then-president of the Screen Actors Guild Ronald Reagan, as a "friendly witness" before the House of Representatives' Un-American Activities Committee. Disney had been deeply stung by union organizers and, later, strikers at his studios, whom he firmly believed were Communist agitators. Under questioning, Disney identified four of his former employees as Communists, though he had no evidence. He then reassured the committee that he was firmly convinced that Walt Disney Studios had been cleansed of any remaining Communist taint.

DISNEY QUIZ

What well-known rocker agreed to play Captain Jack Sparrow's father in the 2006 movie sequel *Pirates of the Caribbean: Dead Man's Chest,* after Johnny Depp said he had modeled the character—eye makeup, long hair, jewelry, and all—on him in the first film?

Rolling Stones guitarist Keith Richards

(1971) Roy O. Disney, who had carried the burden of his brother's dreams for most of his adult life, and certainly for the five years since Walt's death, formally dedicated Walt Disney World to his brother's memory. Although he continued to give his brother the credit—and insisted that "Walt" be added to the name of the park, which had previously been known simply as Disney World—Roy had worked tirelessly since Walt's death to bring the dream to life, raising more than $400 million for the park's construction. Just two months after the dedication, Roy Disney passed away.

October

NAME THAT 'TOON

What film, released in 1939, marked Disney's 75th and last "Silly Symphony"?

"The Ugly Duckling"

26
October

(1971) One of Walt Disney World's most popular attractions, the Electrical Water Pageant, debuted on the Seven Seas Lagoon. Originally known as the Electrical Pageant, it is a thousand-foot-long floating parade, two "trains" of seven barges each bearing 25-foot-tall screens covered in blinking lights. To the sounds of Disney movie music and classical themes, these light silhouettes of sea creatures circle the water every night between 9 and 10. The parade is visible from the Polynesian, Grand Floridian, Wilderness Lodge, Fort Wilderness, and Contemporary hotels; guests often time their dinner reservations to coincide with the free show. The dry-land Main Street Electrical Parade debuted at Disneyland in 1972.

DID YOU KNOW?

Walt Disney intended "Three Little Pigs," as a present to his wife on the occasion of daughter Diane's birth. On Christmas Day 1933, a week after Diane was born, Walt gave Lilly a private viewing in the baby's nursery. According to Disney biographer Leonard Mosley, she assured her husband, "It's the best thing you've ever done! But you know, I somehow feel I ought to have given you . . . triplets!"

27

October

(1954) During the first ABC broadcast of *Walt Disney Presents,* Walt Disney made the first public announcement of the plans for Disneyland. During the show, as part of the promotion for the forthcoming *Davy Crockett* series, Fess Parker sang "The Ballad of Davy Crockett," which went to the top of the charts and stayed there for 13 weeks. The series itself premiered December 15.

(2002) The Anaheim Angels, which had belonged to the Walt Disney Company since 1998, won their first World Series over the San Francisco Giants.

LEGENDARY PEOPLE

What award-winning lyricist responsible for hit songs in *Aladdin, Beauty and the Beast,* and *The Lion King* was knighted by Queen Elizabeth II in 1994, almost a decade before entering Disney's hall of fame?

Sir Tim Rice, named a Disney Legend in 2002

DISNEY QUIZ

Who provided the voice of Mickey Mouse until 1946?

Walt Disney himself

28

October

(1994) *Squanto,* about an American Indian who, after overcoming his desire for revenge against the *Mayflower* settlers who have taken over his now-deserted village, must help them survive in the New World, was released. It starred Adam Beach, one of the first American Indians cast in the lead of a major motion picture. While Beach's casting as Squanto was still notable as a first, Disney had previously cast two other pioneering American Indian actors, Iron Eyes Cody and Chief Dan George, in several TV shows and movie roles.

DID YOU KNOW?

On-screen and in all movie posters, Disney kept the title of *A Bug's Life* uncapitalized, as in *a bug's life.* This style may be a tip of the antennae to a series called *archy and mehitabel,* created by *New York Evening Sun* columnist Don Marquis in 1916, continued for decades in the *New York Tribune* and *Collier's* magazine, and rediscovered in the late 1980s.

29

October

(2002) A Staffordshire bull terrier named Disney ran into the surf off Cape Town, South Africa, in her second attempt to take down a bull seal more than 20 times her weight. Not at all successful, she needed 45 stitches around her head and she nearly lost her tail. Her story would have made a perfect Disney featurette.

(1971) The grand opening of Walt Disney World ceremonies, starring Julie Andrews, Glen Campbell, Jonathan Winters, Bob Hope, and Buddy Hackett, were broadcast as a TV special. One of the best sequences showed Meredith Willson, author and composer of *The Music Man,* leading the parade.

NAME THAT 'TOON

What Disney film featuring ten cartoon shorts introduced Sergei Prokofiev's "Peter and the Wolf" to the world in 1946?

Make Mine Music

DISNEY QUIZ

According to legend, in the animated *The Great Mouse Detective* (1986), what Disney executive and family member is the villain Ratigan—voiced by veteran Vincent Price—a caricature of?

Walt's son-in-law Ron Miller, who Roy Disney had just helped force out as Disney Company president

30

October

(1906) Prolific composer Paul J. Smith III, who won an Academy Award for the score of *Pinocchio* and was nominated for Oscars for the scores of *Cinderella*, *Snow White*, and *Song of the South*, was born in Calumet, Michigan. Among his other Disney scores were *Pollyanna*, *The Shaggy Dog*, *20,000 Leagues Under the Sea*, *The Parent Trap*, and *Swiss Family Robinson*. He also scored dozens of Disney cartoons.

(1963) *The Incredible Journey*, based on the book about two dogs and a Siamese cat who cross the Canadian wilds searching for their owners, was released. When it was remade in 1993, as *Homeward Bound: The Incredible Journey*, the location was changed to the United States.

DID YOU KNOW?

In 1986, the American Society of Mechanical Engineers designated the Disneyland monorail a National Historic Landmark.

(1936) The studios released "The Country Cousin," a version of Aesop's "city mouse, country mouse" tale. "The Country Cousin" was the 63rd of the 75 "Silly Symphonies" released within a decade, and the 5th to win the animated-short Oscar in six years. The titular hero, Abner, is invited by his urbane cousin Monty to leave his home in Podunk for a visit to the city. There Abner discovers the delights of cocktail-party fare and luxurious lodgings. But after some mishaps, including an introduction to alcohol and close encounters with cats and cabs, Abner decides he prefers his boring home.

31
October

DISNEY QUIZ

What were Mickey Mouse's historic first words, uttered in "Karnival Kid" in 1929?

"Hot dog!"

November

Minnie Mouse and Mickey Mouse at Tokyo Disneyland, 2003

1

November

(1936) *Harper's Bazaar* magazine published "Boom Shot of Hollywood" by Janet Flanner—"Genêt" to readers of her columns for the *New Yorker*—in which she described the paradox of a rigidly organized studio creating animated chaos. "With hysteria the seeming law for moviemaking, it's a wonder Mickey and Silly Symphonies succeed in this world at all, since the place where they're made is as sensible as a post office," Flanner wrote. "Law and order reign there. . . . side by side, with Minnie, Madam Clara Cluck, Donald Duck and Elmer the Elephant who, all Rabelaisian in spots but solidly moral at heart, are doubtless easier to get along with than the other big stars in the movie game."

DID YOU KNOW?

To make sure that the combined energy drain of the Rock 'n' Roller Coaster Starring Aerosmith and the adjacent *Twilight Zone* Tower of Terror ride did not take down the power at Disney-MGM Studios, a dedicated power grid was constructed for the Rock 'n' Roller Coaster.

November

(2001) The fourth Disney-Pixar collaboration, *Monsters, Inc.,* was released, and despite some critical ambivalence, the story of the beast under the bed was very popular. In fact, its worldwide gross of $525 million was the record holder until the release of the sixth Disney-Pixar production, *The Incredibles,* three years later. Like several of Disney's blockbuster hits of the 1990s and after, *Monsters* boasted a soundtrack by a major pop composer, in this case Randy Newman, who won the Best Song Oscar for "If I Didn't Have You."

NAME THAT 'TOON

What hit movie, in an original bit of salesmanship, was briefly pulled from theaters between September 1994, when kids went back to school, and November, when the holiday rush began?

The Lion King

DISNEY QUIZ

What kinds of pets does the wealthy Disney character Scrooge McDuck have?

A lemming, a triceratops named Tootsie, and Baron Itzy Bitsy the Flea

(1977) *Pete's Dragon*, a mixed live action–animation musical about a mischievous dragon who causes panic in a Maine fishing village, premiered, although it did not go into general release for six weeks. The film is remembered today primarily for how the somewhat clumsy dragon interacts with the live cast—and as the first major movie role for singer Helen Reddy. Aside from Reddy, *Pete's Dragon* had a reliable comedy team that included Mickey Rooney, Jim Backus, Shelley Winters, and Red Buttons. Only moderately successful, the movie was edited down by nearly 20 minutes when it was reissued in the mid-1980s.

3
November

DID YOU KNOW?

The Country Bears (2002) was the first of three feature films, all released within 18 months, based on Disney theme park attractions, the other two being *The Haunted Mansion*, starring Eddie Murphy, and *Pirates of the Caribbean*, starring Johnny Depp.

4
November

(2005) *Chicken Little,* the seventh and, under the 1994 contract agreement between Disney and Pixar, the last collaboration between the two studios, was released. The marketing slogan of the film was "Chicken Little. Movie Big." Among the voice artists are Patrick Stewart, Don Knotts (his first appearance in a Disney film since 1979's *The Apple Dumpling Gang Rides Again*), and Adam ("Batman") West. Even Garry Marshall, director of such Disney films as *Pretty Woman* and *Runaway Bride,* has a few lines. The starring chicken is voiced by Zach Braff, star of the ABC sitcom *Scrubs.*

DISNEY QUIZ ————————————

What is the clever name of the cartoon production company formed in 1928 by Rudolf Ising and Hugh Harmon, two of Walt Disney's very first employees at Laugh-O-Gram Films in Kansas City?

Harmon-Ising (say it out loud)

5

November

(2004) *The Incredibles* was released, the sixth Disney-Pixar collaboration and the third in a row, following *Finding Nemo* and *Spirited Away*, to win an Academy Award as Best Animated Feature for the studio. This movie about a family with superpowers seemed to have super box office powers as well. In January 2005, the movie won the Annie Award, animation's equivalent of the Oscar, as Best Animated Feature. In February, *The Incredibles* won the Oscar. Also popular with the public, *The Incredibles* grossed $632 million worldwide, easily setting a new record.

LEGENDARY PEOPLE

What famous Hollywood leading man has appeared in a total of 12 Disney films, beginning with *Follow Me, Boys!* at age 15?

Kurt Russell, named a Disney Legend in 1998

6
November

(2005) With the opening ceremonies completed, the *Black Pearl* sailboat headed for Capetown, South Africa, to make preparations before the Volvo Ocean (around-the-world) Race. The 70-foot *Black Pearl* was sponsored by Disney to promote *Pirates of the Caribbean: Dead Man's Chest,* the sequel to its 2003 hit. The film is scheduled to premiere in July 2006, shortly after the end of the race. Disney's commitment was no small potatoes, since just hiring a professional crew for an eight-month race costs about $16 million. Having *Pirates* stars Johnny Depp, Keira Knightley, and Orlando Bloom aboard as crew members (albeit separately and temporarily) upped the ante substantially.

DISNEY QUIZ

In *Toy Story 2,* who provides the voice of Emperor Zurg and Crush the surfer turtle?

Nemo writer-director Andrew Stanton

NAME THAT 'TOON

What cartoon did Walt Disney let Lillian privately view on Christmas Day 1933, a week after their daughter Diane was born?

"Three Little Pigs"

November

(2001) The company announced its acquisition of the Baby Einstein child-education company, which specialized in videos introducing babies to classical music, fine arts, literature, and foreign languages. Details of the all-cash transaction were not made public, but the *Wall Street Journal* estimated it at $25 million—not bad for a mom-and-pop company founded by a former teacher in 1996 with just $5,000. In addition to creating such brand-related merchandise as rattles and plush toys, Disney targeted preschoolers with the plot- and character-driven "Little Einstein" concept the next year. Disney has also launched Baby Einstein in Asia, South America, Europe, and New Zealand.

DID YOU KNOW?

Walt Disney's one-eighth-scale Carolwood-Pacific Railway once broke down with actress Irene Dunne and Hollywood gossip diva Hedda Hopper aboard, both wearing long evening dresses, and they had to walk back from the trestle.

8
November

(1973) *Robin Hood,* a genial, *Aesop's Fables*–like version of the children's classic, was released. Simultaneously celebrating the opening of railroad service to Fort Wilderness, the company invited out-of-town media to Walt Disney World for a medieval banquet in the forest lit by torchlight and accompanied by costumed period musicians.

Like so many Disney films from *Song of the South* to *The Jungle Book,* the animated version of *Robin Hood* showcases the animators' ability to put human characteristics (and foibles) onto animal forms and faces, playing off old puns and legends.

NAME THAT 'TOON ————————————

What Mickey Mouse cartoon first featured the animated farmyard couple Horace Horsecollar and Clarabelle Cow?

"The Plow Boy" (1929)

DISNEY QUIZ ————————————

Who was the first cartoon character ever to be awarded a star along Hollywood's Walk of Fame, on November 18, 1978?

Mickey Mouse

(1999) *Mickey's Once upon a Christmas,* a 70-minute video collection of new holiday shorts, was released. On the fifth anniversary of that film, a sequel named *Mickey's Twice upon a Christmas* was released on video. It was more of a landmark than its predecessor, because for the first time the characters were created by computer software, using technology developed for the 3-D "Mickey's PhilharMagic" film at Disney World. Despite the characters' new interactive look, they sound familiar, thanks to husband and wife team Wayne Allwine and Russi Taylor as Mickey and Minnie, Tony Anselmo as Donald Duck, and Alan Young as Uncle Scrooge.

9
November

DID YOU KNOW?

After the success of *Snow White and the Seven Dwarfs,* film studio carpenters made a replica of the dwarfs' cottage as a Christmas gift for Walt's two daughters. The girls were fascinated for about five minutes, Lillian laughed later, and then became more interested in the box it had come in.

10
November

(1953) *The Living Desert,* the first full-length "True-Life Adventure," was released. It had cost $500,000 to make, but it grossed ten times that; and it won an Academy Award for Best Documentary Feature. It was also the very first film distributed directly by the Disney Company, which had just ended its contract with RKO. RKO had been reluctant to handle the "True-Life" featurettes and was especially skeptical about a full-length nature film. So Walt convinced his brother Roy to begin distributing their productions themselves. Roy set up Buena Vista, which eventually became a permanent fixture of the company.

DISNEY QUIZ ————————————————

During the early excavation of the Disneyland property, landscaper Bill Evans wrapped colored rags around the trees he wanted saved, but upon his return, he found that all the trees had been cut down. Why?

Apparently, the bulldozer operator was color-blind.

November

(1956) Walt Disney—using a very deep voice to avoid a falsetto that might quickly be identified as Mickey Mouse's—was the mystery guest on the popular CBS program *What's My Line?* It was quite the episode, since that night's panel featured a surprise guest, comedian Jerry Lewis, in addition to regular panelists actress Arlene Francis, newspaper columnist Dorothy Kilgallen, and author–Random House publisher Bennett Cerf. After Disney's identity was discovered, there followed a discussion of Disney's still fairly new entry into the television medium and about some recent additions to Disneyland, including the Skyway and Tom Sawyer's Island.

"Observe everything. Communicate well. Draw, draw, draw."

—Animator Frank Thomas,
giving advice to younger animators

NAME THAT 'TOON

In what "Silly Symphony" film did Donald Duck make his very first appearance, as a supporting character?

"The Wise Little Hen" (1934)

12

November

(1946) *Song of the South,* a mixed live-action (70%) and animated feature based on Joel Chandler Harris's Uncle Remus stories, premiered in Atlanta. This was an expensive project (totaling more than $2 million), and nationwide it was not a financial success. Though now considered to exploit antebellum stereotypes, the movie has begun to regain its good reputation. Regardless of content, *Song of the South* shows Disney animation at its best and marks the beginning of the studios' "middle period." The song "Zip-a-Dee-Doo-Dah" won an Academy Award, and James Baskett received an honorary Oscar for his portrayal of Uncle Remus.

DISNEY QUIZ

Which character in *Pinocchio* is said to be a caricature of gifted animator Fred Moore?

Lampwick

DID YOU KNOW?

Walt Disney didn't invent his own "signature," that now-familiar clear "W" and "D." It was created by studio artists as a graphic logo.

(1991) *Beauty and the Beast,* the first animated feature nominated for the Best Picture Academy Award, premiered in New York City. The film was nominated in six categories, although it won for only two, Best Song and Best Score. This movie score was the last one completed by the team of Howard Ashman and Alan Menken; in March, already in the midst of scoring *Aladdin,* Ashman died. *Beauty* had been a massive undertaking, lasting three and a half years and involving nearly 600 artists and animators. At $140 million, it became the most successful animated feature in history at that time.

13
November

NAME THAT 'TOON

What Disney-Pixar collaboration tells the story of an overprotective father who, accompanied by a pelican, a vegan shark, some surfer-dude sea turtles, and a vague but good-hearted royal blue tang, sets out to rescue his six-year-old son whose been kidnapped from Australia's Great Barrier Reef?

Finding Nemo (2003)

14
November

(2002) The image of Mickey Mouse appeared in a fresco on the outside of a small Catholic church in Malta, Austria. The fresco, dating to the 14th century, was being restored when the image of a creature with two round ears and a laughing mouth was uncovered. (Although it would not strike younger audiences so strongly, it does resemble the earlier, less all-round Mickey.)

The fresco is in fact a portrayal of Saint Christopher, who was often seen with a retinue of fabulous characters and who is sometimes described as having a dog's head, so "Mickey" might even be an alternate portrait of the saint.

DISNEY QUIZ ————————————————

What three theme park vessels are named in honor of Lillian Disney, Walt's wife?

The riverboat *Empress Lilly* (now Fulton's Crab House at Pleasure Island), the *Lilly Belle* locomotive at Disney World, and the *Lilly Belle* VIP caboose at Disneyland

(1989) *The Little Mermaid* premiered in New York and Los Angeles. Called by the *New York Times* "the best animated Disney film in 30 years," *The Little Mermaid* grossed more than $222 million worldwide. *Mermaid* was the first Disney project in which Howard Ashman and Alan Menken were involved. Ashman, who became the film's coproducer, took the lead in shaping the script, turning Ursula the sea witch into a caricature of transvestite cult star Divine and Ariel into more of a valley girl than the traditional Disney princess. Ashman and Menken won Oscars for Best Song ("Under the Sea") and Best Score.

15
November

DID YOU KNOW?

In trying to build his Carolwood-Pacific Railway exactly to scale, one day Walt Disney called the prop office, according to Lilly, and said, "Boys, I want you to find me a few human beings, one-eighth-scale, to ride the train." Accustomed to offbeat searches, the staff replied, "Okay, Walt, we'll try"—and then did a double take. Walt cracked up laughing.

16
November

(1990) *The Rescuers Down Under,* the first animated film created specifically as a sequel and the first film in which computer technology replaced the hand-painting of cels, was released. For this film, there were, in fact, no cels at all. CAPS, for Computer Animation Production System, allowed the animators' hand drawings to be copied and colored electronically and to be produced on video instead of celluloid. It also let characters and backgrounds be manipulated in more ways so as to create a more realistic three-dimensional look, replacing the multiplane camera that had been one of Walt Disney's most important inventions.

DID YOU KNOW? ——————————————

Olympic ice skater Michelle Kwan has made almost annual Disney-themed television specials since 1999, beginning with "Michelle Kwan Skates to Disney's Greatest Hits."

BY THE NUMBERS ——————————————

More than 8,000 acres at Walt Disney World have been designated as permanent wildlife conservation areas and will never be developed.

(1973) Walt Disney World was the site of one of the most famous moments in American political history: here, during a televised hour-long question-and-answer session with 400 managing editors of Associated Press bureaus, then-President Richard M. Nixon uttered "I am not a crook." Nixon repeated his version of the events of the previous year and declared, "[The American] people have got to know whether or not their president is a crook. Well, I'm not a crook." Nixon was impeached on July 27, 1974, and again on July 29 and 30. On August 8, 1974, he announced his resignation.

17

November

DISNEY QUIZ

According to some Vin Diesel fans, what Disney character appears as a tattoo on the action star's bicep in the film *xXx*?

Ferdinand the Bull (although some say it is the astrological sign Taurus)

18

November

(1928) "Steamboat Willie" had its debut at the Colony Theater in New York City. Although not really the first Mickey Mouse cartoon—it was the third one finished—this marked Mickey's first cartoon appearance to the public, and so this date is considered his official birthday.

Mickey was an instant hit. Disney released 11 Mickey Mouse films in 1929, 9 in 1930, 12 in 1931, 14 in 1932, and 12 in 1933. In 1932, the Academy of Motion Picture Arts and Sciences awarded Walt Disney a special Oscar in recognition of Mickey's creation.

DID YOU KNOW?

When the Lionel model train company filed for bankruptcy in the mid-1930s, a judge allowed them to produce a Mickey and Minnie handcar for that Christmas, and the revenues were enough to wipe out the red ink.

(1999) *Toy Story 2*, one of the few sequels in history to exceed the original in sales, debuted at a special premiere at Hollywood's El Capitan. Still the fourth-biggest-grossing movie in Disney history, it earned close to $500 million worldwide. The video release set records of its own, helped by the hilarious "outtakes" that have the animated cast muffing their lines as if they were real actors.

(2004) Disney released *National Treasure*, starring Nicholas Cage. Riding the coattails of the *Da Vinci Code* craze, *National Treasure* launched rumors that some of the nation's historical documents had been stolen. Eventually, it was admitted that the National Archives had indeed been the victim of document theft.

19
November

DISNEY QUIZ

What is Mickey Mouse's official birthday?

November 18, 1928, the release date of "Steamboat Willie"

November

(1998) *A Bug's Life,* the second Disney-Pixar collaboration, premiered in Los Angeles. It went into general release on November 25, eventually grossing $364 million worldwide. Like *Toy Story* before it, *A Bug's Life* was entirely computer-animated, taking advantage of the computer's ability to replicate natural forms to fill the screen with a miniature universe of leaves, insects, and sky.

Even before hitting video in 1999, *A Bug's Life* had inspired one of the most intriguing attractions in Disney World's Animal Kingdom. The 3-D It's Tough To Be a Bug, which plays in a theater beneath the Tree of Life, opened in April 1998.

BY THE NUMBERS

What was the generous beginning salary earned by Tim Considine and David Stollery when they signed on in 1955 to play Spin and Marty in *The Adventures of Spin and Marty?*

$400 per week

(1994) *Honey, I Shrunk the Audience*, a 3-D film attraction in the Journey into Imagination pavilion at Epcot's Future World, opened, replacing the star-studded "Captain Eo." Based on the popular 1989 film, and again starring Rick Moranis in the role of Professor Wayne Szalinski, *Honey* replays the special effects game on the audience by super-sizing a hungry python, a dog (who sneezes on the audience), and so on. There is also a giant-scaled playground at the Disney-MGM Studios nearby called Honey, I Shrunk the Kids Movie Adventure.

21
November

DISNEY QUIZ

What former Disney animator do the haunted mansions at Disneyland and Tokyo Disneyland salute when they shift to a "Nightmare before Christmas" theme at holiday time?

Tim Burton

DID YOU KNOW?

The Ingersoll-Waterbury Company was on the verge of collapse before the advent of the Mickey Mouse watch in 1933.

November

(1942) Annette Funicello, probably the most famous Mouseketeer of all time, was born in Utica, New York. Annette's cherubic curls and precocious curves made her a teenage heart-throb, albeit an all-American one. Walt Disney himself discovered her at an amateur-hour show in the Burbank Starlight Bowl. In addition to performing as a Mouseketeer, she appeared in many Disney movies and TV films, notably *Babes in Toyland* and *The Shaggy Dog*. In 1987 she disclosed that she was suffering from multiple sclerosis. A film bio called *A Dream Is a Wish Your Heart Makes,* based on her autobiography, was released in 1995.

DID YOU KNOW? ————————————

Walt Disney's first Hollywood job almost diverted him from cartooning. He was supposed to have a walk-on as an extra on a Western, but it rained and by the time the scene could be shot, he had been replaced. "That was the end of my career as an actor," he remarked.

(1952) Fred Moore, probably the greatest influence on Mickey Mouse after Walt Disney and Ub Iwerks, died from internal bleeding a day after a car accident. Immensely gifted, Moore began working for Walt as a teenager in 1930 and served as animator or animating director for most of the major films from *Snow White* to *Peter Pan*. Known among animators as the "Mickey expert," Moore not only altered Mickey's looks—making the body pear-shaped rather than round and putting pupils in his eyes—but also wrote directions about changing Mickey's body to go along with emotions and action.

23
November

DISNEY QUIZ

What was the URL address for animation head Roy E. Disney and investor Stanley Gold's anti-Eisner Web site, which they agreed to shut down in August 2005?

www.SaveDisney.com

24
November

(1955) The Mickey Mouse Club Circus debuted at Disneyland. Walt Disney had visited circuses and carnivals while working out the plan for Disneyland, and a Disneyland circus seemed to fit right into that Main Street nostalgia. So he had an old-fashioned circus tent rigged, beneath which athletic Mouseketeers rode horses, swung from trapezes, or tumbled and mugged as clowns. Yet the big top didn't attract big audiences, since families intent on circling the park were not interested in sitting still for even a star-studded circus. The Mickey Mouse Club Circus closed January 8, after only about six weeks.

DISNEY QUIZ

According to the Disneyland attraction's backstory, who once owned the Haunted Mansion?

Master Gracey (after Imagineer Yale Gracey)

DID YOU KNOW?

According to Disney archivist Dave Smith, Walt Disney was first intrigued by the concept of audio-animatronics during a visit to New Orleans, where he found an old windup mechanical bird in an antiques shop.

25
November

(1938) "Ferdinand the Bull," based on the international book by Munro Leaf, was released. It would win an Academy Award for Best Cartoon Short, making that the seventh year in a row Disney would receive an Oscar in this category. "Ferdinand" was up against three other Disney titles—"The Brave Little Tailor" with Mickey Mouse, "Good Scouts" with Donald Duck, and a "Silly Symphony" called "Mother Goose Goes Hollywood." About a tenderhearted bovine who refuses to fight in the bullring, "Ferdinand" was a popular bit of world-peace propaganda (especially considering it was released during the Spanish Civil War).

NAME THAT 'TOON

What 2003 animated film, the result of a 1946 collaboration between Salvador Dalí and Walt Disney, depicts a ballerina who moves through a dreamlike landscape full of such Dalí icons as a melting watch, a cactus, the Tower of Babel, classical ruins, and oversize insects?

Destino

26
November

(1971) On the day after Thanksgiving, less than two months after Walt Disney World's opening, so many people flocked there that parking reached capacity and entry had to be restricted for several hours. The holiday timing was not a fluke: the same thing happened on December 27 and 28; attendance on December 29 neared 70,000. In 1973, the high point shifted to Easter but went back to Christmas in 1974. By 1975, the New Year's Eve crowd was 82,404, a record broken on December 28, 1977.

(1998) "Winnie the Pooh: Thanksgiving" aired as an ABC special, a couple of weeks after the longer *Winnie the Pooh: Seasons of Giving* was released as an original video.

DISNEY QUIZ —————————————————

What kind of statue did Walt Disney receive when he was honored with a special award for *Snow White and the Seven Dwarfs* at the 1939 Oscars?

One regular-size Oscar statuette and seven miniature ones

(1995) At the end of the first weekend of the Osborne Family Spectacle of Lights at Disney-MGM Studios in Orlando, a major tradition had been established. The display began in 1986 as a Christmas present from Arkansas businessman Jennings Osborne to his six-year-old daughter. As the display grew to nearly three million lights, the Osbornes faced not only neighbors angry about the bright lights and traffic but also lawsuits. That's when Disney executives purchased the exhibit. Nowadays, it totals almost five million lights and takes ten weeks to install. The Osborne family still comes to "visit" their lights each year.

November

WHERE'S MICKEY?

After Sarah Jessica Parker, whose fashion style on *Sex and the City* made her a pop-culture icon, wore a Mickey T-shirt under a white tux jacket on the show, a Hollywood boutique reported selling out its 60 shirts within days.

28
November

(1995) The Walt Disney Speedway, a one-mile race track created out of a corner of the Magic Kingdom parking lot at Disney World, was officially dedicated. It was broken in by a Formula Ford 200 support race on January 26, 1996, and then the inaugural Indy 200 race on January 27, which rookie Buzz Calkins won.

Since February 1997, the track has been exclusively used by the Richard Petty Driving Experience, a combination driving school and thrill ride in which participants drive a stock car at full speed. Depending on time (and money), motor sport fans can drive as many as 30 laps.

DID YOU KNOW?

Upon seeing the film version of her book *Mary Poppins* at its premiere, author P. T. Travers was horrified by the somewhat haphazard Cockney accent of Dick Van Dyke, the only American actor in the film, and wanted to replace him.

NAME THAT 'TOON

In what early cartoon does Mickey Mouse club members of a cat army over the head with a hammer until the cats retreat and Mickey becomes a hero to the mice of his homeland?

"The Barnyard Battle" (1929)

(1971) The inaugural Walt Disney World PGA Invitational golf tournament was held on the Magnolia and Palm courses. Jack Nicklaus was the winner that year, and also in 1972 and 1973. Since 1973, the tournament has been won by such players as Tiger Woods and Hal Sutton (both twice, and both as rookies), Larry Nelson and John Huston (both also twice), David Duval, Vijay Singh, Lanny Wadkins, Ray Floyd, Jeff Maggert, and Mark O'Meara. For winning that first tournament, Nicklaus took home $30,000; by 2005, the purse had swelled to $4.4 million, with the winner's share totaling more than $750,000.

November

BY THE NUMBERS

The stunt cars in Lights, Motors, Action! Extreme Stunt Show weigh only about 1,300 pounds and consume one quart of fuel per show. Each car has as many reverse gears, four, as forward gears, meaning it can go backwards as fast as forwards. One car actually has two engines, so it can split in half and take off in both directions at once.

> "Disney has the best casting. If he doesn't like an actor he just tears him up."
>
> —*Alfred Hitchcock*

30

November

(1987) It was announced that *Three Men and a Baby* had grossed $10.4 million in its first weekend. The movie would make $170 million and lead to a sequel, *Three Men and a Little Lady*. Starring Tom Selleck, Ted Danson, and Steve Guttenberg, the first film was based on a French comedy called *Trois Hommes et un Couffin* (*Three Men and a Cradle*) that Disney CEO Michael Eisner had seen while in Paris in 1985 to meet with Prime Minister Jacques Chirac about building France's Disney park. Eisner instantly wanted to buy the rights and wound up paying an unprecedented $1 million.

DID YOU KNOW? ————————————————

One of the most famous poster visuals of the *Lion King* movie, with Simba and Nala posing atop a cliff as Rafiki holds up their cub, never appears in the film. It combines a picture of the adult lions from near the end of the film with a bit of Rafiki holding up the baby Simba in the beginning.

December

Roy Disney and Mickey Mouse, 1999, in Pasadena, California

1
December

(1966) *Follow Me, Boys!,* which starred Fred MacMurray and featured a 14-year-old actor whom Walt Disney had already signed to a ten-year contract, was released. Kurt Russell made nine films in those first ten years, including *The Computer Wore Tennis Shoes, The Barefoot Executive,* and *The Strongest Man in the World;* and he continued to act and provide voices, including Copper in *The Fox and the Hound,* for Disney thereafter. Nearly 40 years later, Kurt Russell would still be starring in movies for the Disney Company, specifically as the superhero father Steve Stronghold in *Sky High* (2005).

DISNEY QUIZ ————————————

Whose faces appear on the $1, $5, $10, and $50 bills of Disney Dollars?

Dumbo or Cinderella appear on the $1 bill, Goofy or Donald on the $5, Minnie Mouse or Stitch on the $10, and Mickey Mouse on the $50.

December

(1929) "The Haunted House," which has Mickey Mouse taking shelter from the storm in what turns out to be a well-populated mansion, was released. "Haunted House" marked the first time the animators created what would become a popular Disney setting: the ghost-filled mansion. This one even had a huge pipe organ, a nod to Lon Chaney's hugely popular 1925 silent *Phantom of the Opera*, and an instrument that would become a fixture in haunted-house settings ever after.

NAME THAT 'TOON

What Oscar-nominated Disney cartoon short explains the real story behind the nursery rhyme "Mary, Mary, Quite Contrary," which is actually about Queen Mary Tudor, also known as Bloody Mary, who tried to return Britain to Catholicism?

"The Truth about Mother Goose" (1957)

DID YOU KNOW?

According to Bob Penfield, who was assigned to King Arthur's Carrousel in the early days of Disneyland, the fountains choked and fell short because of an apparent water shortage. "There had been a plumbing shortage," said Penfield, "and Walt had to choose between toilets and fountains."

3

December

(1947) On or about this day, Scrooge McDuck, the uncle of Donald Duck and legendarily "the richest duck in the world," made his first appearance in a story called "Christmas on Bear Mountain" in Disney's "Four-Color" comics. Scrooge was perhaps the most famous creation of artist Carl Barks, himself the most famous of all Disney comic book artists. Scrooge had his own series of comics beginning in March 1952 but did not make his debut in an animated cartoon until 1967, in "Scrooge McDuck and Money." He also starred in the TV series *Duck Tales* beginning in September 1987.

"In learning the art of storytelling by animation, I have discovered that language has an anatomy. Every spoken word, whether uttered by a living person or by a cartoon character, has its facial grimace, emphasizing the meaning."

—Walt Disney

(1918) Walt Disney arrived in Le Havre, France, on the SS *Vaubin*. From there he took a train to Saint-Cyr, where he celebrated his 17th birthday. Walt had hoped to follow his brother Roy into the navy, but he was too young. So he joined the American Ambulance Corps. Yet this was the year of the influenza epidemic that killed tens of millions worldwide, and Walt caught the flu. By the time he got well the war was over, but he was accepted for recovery work. He stayed in France for only eight months before returning to Kansas City to make it as an artist.

4
December

DISNEY QUIZ

In *Fantasia/2000,* what celebrated musician solos on "Pines of Rome," which becomes a sort of dance of the whales?

Itzhak Perlman

LEGENDARY PEOPLE

What star of the Disney movies *Father of the Bride* and *Bringing Down the House* began developing some of his trademark comedy tricks while working at Disneyland's old Merlin's Magic Shop as a teenager?

Steve Martin, named a Disney Legend in 2005

5
December

(1901) Walter Elias Disney was born in Chicago, the youngest of four sons, and the next to last child. When Walt was five, his family moved to Marceline, Missouri. Even though he spent only about four years there, Walt considered it his hometown and had it in mind when envisioning the Main Street at his parks.

According to family legend, Walt started doodling almost as soon as he could walk. As a boy, he drew a portrait of the local doctor's buggy stallion and sold it to him for 50 cents, and as a teenager, he paid his Kansas City barber in cartoons.

DISNEY QUIZ

Why is July 17, 1955, often referred to as Black Sunday in Disney circles?

The evening before it opened to the public on July 18, Disneyland hosted an invitation-only opening ceremony, but thousands of tickets were counterfeited, and instead of 22,000 guests, more than 30,000 people showed up. Food ran short, parking was jammed, and there was a natural-gas leak in Fantasyland. Fountains choked, and rides broke down.

WHERE'S MICKEY?

After rocker Lenny Kravitz was photographed in 2001 wearing his vintage Disney shirt, online auctions and preowned-clothing stores began selling them at prices up to $300.

6

December

(1903) Ruth Flora Disney, the youngest of Walt's siblings and one of his favorites, was born in Chicago. Ruth was the inspiration for Walt's very first bit of animation art: when he was age nine and she was age seven, she caught the measles, and he made her a cartoon booklet that she flipped to watch the figures move. She was the only other of Walt's and Roy's siblings to work at the Disney studios, joining up in the summer of 1925.

DID YOU KNOW?

Traditionally a popular day for Disney movie releases, Christmas Day has seen the release of *Old Yeller* in 1957, *Tonka* in 1958, *The Sword in the Stone* in 1963, *Tombstone* in 1993, the live-action *Jungle Book* in 1994, *Evita* in 1996, *Mighty Joe Young* in 1998, *The Shipping News* in 2001, the reconfigured IMAX version of *The Lion King* in 2002, *The Young Black Stallion* and *Cold Mountain* in 2003, and *The Aviator* in 2004.

7

December

(1964) Compass East Corporation, one of the firms that Walt and Roy Disney used as fronts to acquire the land for Walt Disney World, was established in Delaware. If the public knew the Disneys were buying up real estate, landowners would triple their asking prices. So Roy and Walt worked behind the scenes. The first large purchase involved state senator Irlo "Bud" Bronson, who sold them 8,400 acres of scrub and swamp for just over $100 an acre. In the end, the brothers acquired Disney World for less than $185 an acre; within months the surrounding land would be selling for $40,000–$250,000 an acre.

BY THE NUMBERS

In 2005, the Walt Disney Company donated more than $190 million in cash, in-kind donations, and airtime to charities and relief organizations, while Disney VoluntEARS performed more than 442,000 hours of community service.

(1941) The day after the Japanese launched a surprise attack on Pearl Harbor, President Franklin Delano Roosevelt declared the nation at war, and the U.S. Army commandeered Disney's soundstage on Hyperion Avenue. It was not Disney's filmmaking equipment the army needed—though that would eventually be put to use—but rather the warehouse space for repairing antiaircraft guns. Only blocks from the Lockheed aircraft plant, Disney's location turned out to be unexpectedly strategic, and within hours of the catastrophe, 700 soldiers had taken over the Disney studios. They bivouacked in the offices for some eight months.

8
December

DISNEY QUIZ

In *Fantasia/2000,* what classical piece is heard while a flock of naturally gawky flamingos yo-yo?

Saint-Saëns's "Carnival of the Animals"

NAME THAT 'TOON

What animated film features two villainous henchmen named Pain and Panic?

Hercules (1997)

9

December

(1992) The National Hockey League awarded the California expansion team to the Disney Company, which named them the Mighty Ducks after the movie released months earlier. The movie netted about $50 million, just the amount needed to buy the team. Half the $50 million went for franchise fees; the other half was awarded against prospective losses to the Los Angeles Kings. Disney anted up another $600 million for NHL broadcast rights. In the 2002–03 season, the Ducks won the Western Division to get into the Stanley Cup finals. Despite their success, in 2005 it was announced that the team would be sold— reportedly for $75 million.

DISNEY QUIZ

What three celebrity hosts of the live TV broadcast of Disneyland's opening ceremonies on July 17, 1955, returned in January 1990 to help kick off Disneyland's 35th-anniversary season?

Art Linkletter (incidentally celebrating his own birthday), Robert Cummings, and Ronald Reagan

(1941) Original Mouseketeer Tommy Kirk was born in Louisville, Kentucky. He was spotted acting at age 13 and signed to *The Mickey Mouse Club* in 1955. Over the next ten years he starred in *The Hardy Boys* series and such hit films as *Old Yeller* and *Swiss Family Robinson*. After Disney executives discovered he was gay, he was released from the Disney studios and was generally blacklisted by Hollywood.

10
December

(1985) Another child star, Raven, star of Disney's TV series *Hangin' with Mr. Cooper* and *That's So Raven* and the voice of Monique in the animated series *Kim Possible*, was born in Atlanta, Georgia.

DID YOU KNOW?

Even though they were among the Disney brothers' first employees—and suffered the worst fears when times were tight—Walt's and Roy's wives, Lillian and Edna, were not named Disney Legends until 2003.

11

December

(1970) *The Aristocats,* the first full-length animation project completed without Walt Disney's participation, premiered in New York and Los Angeles. It went into general release two weeks later and proved a popular success. Walt had given this project, a sort of cross between a feline *Lady and the Tramp* and *101 Dalmatians,* the green light before he died. More than 35 animators worked over four years, creating 350,000 drawings. And the movie had an unusually accomplished cast, including Eva Gabor, Scatman Crothers, Phil Harris, Paul Winchell, Thurl Ravenscroft, Sterling Holloway, and even Maurice Chevalier, who sang the title song.

NAME THAT 'TOON

What film's heroine has a partner in misadventure called Mushu (as in mu shu pork), voiced by Eddie Murphy?

Mulan (1998)

LEGENDARY PEOPLE

Who made history as the Disney studios' first female animator, credited on-screen for her work on the 1942 classic *Bambi?*

Retta Scott, named a Disney Legend in 2000

(1941) "7 Wise Dwarfs," using the popular dwarfs to persuade Canadian citizens to participate in the war effort by buying bonds, was delivered to the National Film Board of Canada. Disney had submitted a similar propaganda film to the board a month earlier. "The Thrifty Pig," borrowing from "The Three Little Pigs," turned the Big Bad Wolf into a Nazi and the third pig's brick home into a construction of Canadian war bonds.

(1981) *Walt Disney—One Man's Dream* aired as a two-hour TV movie. Christian Hoff was the young Walt Disney, marking the first time anyone had played Walt except Walt himself.

12
December

DID YOU KNOW?

The otter couple that starred in *Wonderful World of Disney* shows "An Otter in the Family" and "A Day in Teton Marsh" were raised by a Cajun naturalist and professional snake handler named "Alligator Annie" Miller, who founded the first swamp boat-tour business in Louisiana and was largely responsible for persuading the state to create alligator preserves in the bayous.

13

December

(1925) Dick Van Dyke, the only American actor in the cast of *Mary Poppins,* was born. Van Dyke once wondered why Walt Disney had chosen him for the role of Bert, the London chimney sweep and sometime sidewalk artist. Walt later admitted that he had never seen Van Dyke on television until one of the casting crew recommended him. Disney tuned into *The Dick Van Dyke Show* and was immediately sure he had his man.

In 1966, Van Dyke starred in *Lt. Robin Crusoe, USN,* and later narrated *Walt Disney— One Man's Dream* for TV.

BY THE NUMBERS ———

Each year, guests at the Disneyland park alone consume more than 4 million hamburgers, 1.6 million hot dogs, and—evidence of its large Hispanic audience—2.8 million churros. Walt Disney World guests chow down on 7 million hamburgers, 5 million hot dogs, and 1.4 million barbecued turkey legs.

(1961) *Babes in Toyland,* Disney's first live-action musical, was released. Its climactic scene, in which the wooden soldiers march and toy airships take flight, was considered a classic example of early special effects. Ward Kimball, who collected vintage toys, headed up the mechanical design team.

14
December

Based on the Victor Herbert operetta and tuned up by Disney stable composers George Bruns and Mel Leven, *Babes* is a Mother Goose goof starring Annette Funicello as Mary Contrary and Tommy Sands as Tom Piper, Ann Jillian as Bo Peep, Ed Wynn as the Toymaker, and *Oz* scarecrow Ray Bolger as the villain Barnaby.

DISNEY QUIZ

What prize did 5- and 7-year-old cousins Kristine Vess and Michael Schwartner and 22-year-old Dave MacPherson receive for being the first two children and the first adult to enter Disneyland on July 18, 1955?

They each got lifetime passes for four to Disneyland—later expanded to cover Walt Disney World and Disneyland Paris.

15

December

(1966) Walt Disney, just past his 65th birthday, died of complications from lung cancer at St. Joseph's Hospital in Burbank. The flags along Disneyland's Main Street were lowered to half-mast. He was cremated two days later and buried in Forest Lawn Cemetery.

The night before he died, Walt called chief of operations Joe Fowler into his hospital room, raised his arm like a paintbrush toward the ceiling, and drew the outline of his dream park, just beginning to take shape in the Florida wetlands. "The last draft of what is now Disney World was sketched out, figuratively, on that ceiling," Fowler later recalled.

DISNEY QUIZ —————————————

In the original *Fantasia*, Mickey climbs the podium to shake hands with legendary conductor Leopold Stokowski. In a similar scene in the sequel, *Fantasia/2000*, with what conductor does Mickey shake hands?

James Levine

(1954) The morning after "Davy Crockett—Indian Fighter" premiered on ABC, the nation woke up with a case of log cabin fever. Americans would spend $300 million (in mid-1950s dollars) on coonskin caps and other Davy Crockett–themed merchandise.

The next two programs, "Davy Crockett Goes to Congress" and "Davy Crockett at the Alamo," aired in January and February 1955. All three were rebroadcast before the movie version was released in May. The next year, realizing how popular the character was, Walt Disney authorized two additional shows, which were released as the film *Davy Crockett and the River Pirates* in 1956.

16
December

NAME THAT 'TOON

What animated feature stars a young Hawaiian girl who, in classic Disney fashion, is orphaned?

Lilo and Stitch (2002)

17

December

(1976) The first *Freaky Friday*, starring Barbara Harris and Jodie Foster as the mother and daughter forced magically to walk a mile in each other's shoes, premiered in Los Angeles. A popular and critical success, *Freaky Friday* was the first of many films with the same gimmick, including an equally success-ful 2003 Disney remake featuring Jamie Lee Curtis and Lindsay Lohan.

In the movie *The Saintly Switch*, which aired on *The Wonderful World of Disney* in January 1999, the kids cause a swap between their pro football quarterback dad and their feminist mom—a cross between *Freaky Friday* and *The Parent Trap*.

DID YOU KNOW? ————

When Walt and Lilly Disney built their new home in the Holmby Hills area of Los Angeles, Walt included a projection room and a working soda fountain as well as a half-mile railroad track on which Walt could ride his steam engine.

18
December

(1933) Diane Marie Disney, Walt and Lillian's only biological child and a sometime biographer of her father, was born. In 1937, the Disneys adopted Sharon Mae, who had been born on December 31 of the previous year. However, Sharon was not told that she was not the Disneys' natural daughter, and many biographies and resources do not mention it. Although the children grew up surrounded by Disney mania, it was not until they were in grade school that Diane and Sharon realized that their father was "the" Walt Disney.

BY THE NUMBERS

Each of Disney's cruise ships, the *Magic* and the *Wonder,* desalinize 1,200 tons of seawater into freshwater every day—enough water to supply the residents of Chicago and Houston combined.

DISNEY QUIZ

What is the tallest building at Walt Disney World?

The 199-foot-tall *Twilight Zone* Tower of Terror

19

December

(1925) Robert B. Sherman, who with his brother Richard would write some of Disney's most famous songs, including the (literally) breathtaking "Supercalifragilisticexpialidocious," was born in New York City. Shortly after their first top-ten hit in 1958, "Tall Paul" for Annette Funicello, the Shermans became Disney staff songwriters and composed "It's a Small World" for the New York World's Fair. The brothers composed the songs for *The Parent Trap, The Jungle Book,* "Winnie the Pooh and the Honey Tree," and *Mary Poppins,* among other films. In all, they wrote more than 200 songs for 27 films and as many TV productions.

"Mickey Mouse...is always there—he's part of my life. That really is something not everyone can call their claim to fame."

—Annette Funicello

(1924) Sam McKim, the artist who drew the original souvenir maps of Disneyland, was born in British Columbia. Over the years, McKim's conceptual drawings helped his fellow Imagineers create many of the attractions at the 1964–65 New York World's Fair and at Disneyland and Epcot. For example, his sketches provided the groundwork for It's a Small World, the Haunted Mansion, the Carousel of Progress, Great Moments with Mr. Lincoln, and even the monorail.

December **20**

DISNEY QUIZ

According to the fictional legend behind *The Twilight Zone* Tower of Terror attraction, what was the date that lightning tragically struck an elevator carrying some of the hotel's patrons up to the Tip Top Club on the 13th floor and sent them to their death?

October 31, 1929—Halloween night

NAME THAT 'TOON

What early film features Mickey playing piano, chickens circling in an Apache war dance, and, in a twist on the old phrase "It ain't over till the fat lady sings," a pig—believed to be comic strip character Patricia Pig—singing opera?

"Mickey's Follies" (1929)

21

December

(1937) *Snow White and the Seven Dwarfs*, the first full-length animated feature, had a star-studded premiere at the Cathay Circle Theater in Hollywood, with such guests as Charlie Chaplin, Judy Garland, and Clark Gable. Calling it "Disney's Folly," industry experts had predicted *Snow White* would bankrupt Disney—again. It wound up costing three times Walt's initial estimate of $500,000. The 83-minute film required 120,000 initial drawings, another 120,000 in ink, and then those painted with watercolors. More than 750 artists worked for more than three years, including 300 added in 1935 alone. In the end, the expense and labor were justified, as *Snow White* grossed $8.5 million and turned out to be the studios' salvation.

DID YOU KNOW? ————————

After Walt Disney lost control of his animated creation Oswald the Lucky Rabbit to Universal Pictures in March 1928, it took nearly 80 years for the Disney Company to regain the rights to "Mickey Mouse's older brother," as newspaper reports put it. On February 9, 2006, it was announced that NBC-Universal would hand Oswald over to Disney as part of a trade for former ESPN sportscaster Al Michaels.

(1996) Oscar-winning actress Sally Field made her directorial debut with a two-hour TV movie called *The Christmas Tree*. In the movie, Rockefeller Center's head gardener (Andrew McCarthy), who is charged with finding the perfect tree for the famous plaza's annual display, discovers that a convent has the finest specimen he could desire. But the convent's own gardener, played by Julie Harris, has a special attachment to that tree and is unwilling to part with it. Finally, the two gardeners make friends, and he not only gets the tree but also persuades the nun to travel to New York for the grand lighting ceremony.

22
December

WHERE'S MICKEY? ——

On display each holiday season at Disney-MGM Studios in Orlando, the Osborne Family Spectacle of Lights has several "hidden Mickeys" along the way: in the third "puff of smoke" from the train's engine, on some house windows, and on the back face of the clock tower.

DISNEY QUIZ ——

Who were Disneyland's first residents?

Dolly and Owen Pope. They moved into a trailer near the studios the Sunday after Thanksgiving in 1951, and began to raise and train the first horses for the theme park.

23
December

(1954) *20,000 Leagues under the Sea,* the first feature filmed in CinemaScope and one of Disney's finest films, was released. With Walt Disney himself supervising the writing, the script, based on Jules Verne's novel, took more than a year to polish. The film had an impressive cast, including James Mason as the radical genius Captain Nemo, Paul Lukas as the nautical-history professor, Kirk Douglas as the harpoonist Ned Land, and Peter Lorre as the professor's nervous assistant. *20,000 Leagues* cost more than $4 million to make but later won Oscars for Best Special Effects and Art and Set Decoration.

DISNEY QUIZ —————————————————————

What is the name of Donald Duck's little-known twin sister?

Della Thelma

NAME THAT 'TOON—————————————————————

What film, based on a novel by Daniel Mannix, focuses on a puppy named Copper and a young orphaned fox called Tod who grow up as four-legged brothers?

The Fox and the Hound (1981)

(1937) The studio released "Lonesome Ghosts," a precursor (or premonition) of *Ghostbusters* featuring Mickey, Donald, and Goofy as inept exterminators hired by a group of ghosts who expect to have fun frightening them away. The would-be exorcists end up scaring the heck out of the spirits, and the spirits out of the house.

24
December

(1954) "Siam," one of the 17 "People and Places" featurettes released between 1953 and 1960, was released. This travelogue includes a look at the everyday lives of Siam's residents; their classical dance; and a tour of the canals of Bangkok, once known as "the Venice of the Orient."

BY THE NUMBERS

The dragon Maleficent in Disney-MGM Studios' "Fantasmic!" light and laser spectacular weighs more than 32,000 pounds; the 80-foot-long *Steamboat Willie* ship weighs more than twice that.

December

(1957) *Old Yeller*, one of the company's most enduring tearjerkers, was released. Based on the children's book by Fred Gipson, the film grossed $8 million the first time around and was rereleased twice, in 1965 and 1974, before being allowed out on video. The cast came straight out of the Disney star stable: *Davy Crockett's* Fess Parker; Dorothy McGuire, who played the mothers in *Swiss Family Robinson* and *Summer Magic* as well as in *Old Yeller;* the ubiquitous and seemingly inseparable child actors Tommy Kirk and Kevin Corcoran as brothers Travis and Arliss; and "Spike" in the title role.

BY THE NUMBERS ————————————

Hong Kong Disneyland opened on September 12, 2005, at 1 p.m., a time determined by feng shui rules to make sure the park was in harmony with natural forces.

DISNEY QUIZ ————————————

In the images of TV star Rod Serling shown throughout *The Twilight Zone* Tower of Terror attraction, what real prop has been electronically erased?

Serling's trademark cigarette

(1938) The *Lux Radio Theater* aired a dramatization of "Snow White and the Seven Dwarfs," the first of four Disney hits to be re-created for the listening audience during the golden age of radio. All airing in different years on the Monday closest to Christmas, "Pinocchio" was dramatized in 1939, "Alice in Wonderland" on Christmas Eve 1951, and "Peter Pan" in 1953. The shows were broadcast on the NBC Blue Network, which, decades later, would evolve into the ABC network and be bought by the Disney Company. The *Lux Radio Theater* ended its long run in 1955.

26
December

DID YOU KNOW?

It has been reported that many of the skeletons at Disneyland's original Pirates of the Caribbean attraction are real, and that the skull and crossbones mounted over the bed in the Captain's Quarters is a genuine pirate flag Walt Disney received as a gift.

27

December

(1937) Walt Disney appeared on the cover of *Time* magazine, playing with a set of miniature dwarfs and keyed to a feature called "Man and Mouse," which hailed the just-released *Snow White and the Seven Dwarfs* as "the most ambitious animated cartoon ever attempted." The cover caption read, "Happy, Grumpy, Bashful, Sneezy, Sleepy, Doc, Dopey, Disney."

(1954) Exactly 17 years later, Walt again appeared on *Time*. The magazine nicknamed him "Father Goose," and the cover story began with an anecdote about a police officer deep in the Belgian Congo who suddenly encountered the frightening apparition of "Mikimus"— a witch doctor in a Mickey Mouse costume.

DID YOU KNOW?

The 68,000-square-foot building that houses the Rock 'n' Roller Coaster Starring Aerosmith was built around the roller coaster, not beforehand.

28

December

(2001) Marking the 100th anniversary of the year of Walt Disney's birth, the Laughing Place, a prominent Web site for Disney fans, interviewed former Disney artists, voice actors, movie critics, and Imagineers. John Hench started as a story man in 1939, created artwork for *Fantasia* and *Alice in Wonderland,* and became one of the first Imagineers. Asked why so many people felt such attachment to Walt Disney, Hench answered that "Walt was absolutely honest and he never said anything he didn't believe. And I think that somehow that projected from the television."

NAME THAT 'TOON

What early cartoon shows Mickey Mouse falling asleep while reading a book identified as *Through the Looking-Glass* and then having adventures with unfriendly flying decks of cards?

"Thru the Mirror" (1936)

29
December

(2000) One of the studios' most unexpected successes, *O Brother, Where Art Thou?* was released, a week after limited premieres in Los Angeles and New York and more than six months after an initial premiere at the Cannes Film Festival. Created by Ethan and Joel Coen and starring George Clooney, *O Brother* retells the *Odyssey* in the Depression-weary South. The film's soundtrack became by far the most influential folk recording in decades. Almost entirely on word of mouth, it sold five million copies, hit number one on the Billboard charts, and won five Grammys and two Country Music Awards.

"Our greatest natural resource is the minds of our children."

—*Walt Disney*

BY THE NUMBERS —————————————

It took costume makers 100,000 hours and more than 5,500 yards of fabric to create the 125 costumes for the theme park musical show *Cinderellabration.*

(1928) "The Gallopin' Gaucho," which had been in the can for several months and should have been Mickey Mouse's second cartoon, was finally released. Like its predecessor, "Plane Crazy," it didn't find a distributor until after "Steamboat Willie" had become a hit, and after both "Plane Crazy" and "Gallopin' Gaucho" had been dubbed with sound. The film showed what would have been Mickey and Minnie's first meeting, if the cartoons had been released in order. It also marked the first appearance of Black Pete, later "Peg Leg Pete" or plain old "Pete," as Mickey's rival for Minnie's affection.

30
December

DID YOU KNOW? ———————————————

Donald's miserly billionaire uncle Scrooge McDuck is said to be fluent in Arabic, Dutch, German, Mongolian, Spanish, Mayan, and various Chinese dialects as well as English (and, presumably, Duck).

31
December

(1999) *Fantasia/2000*, which had premiered at New York's Carnegie Hall on December 15, got its Hollywood-style coming out at a New Year's Eve gala in Pasadena. It opened in 100 70mm IMAX-format theaters the next day and then went into general release in June 2000.

In the beginning of 2000, the audience sees a collage of images from the older film spinning off into space. Then, as in the first, one hears the musicians tuning up while watching the animators sharpening pencils (their instruments). Among the celebrities lending their voices to 2000 are Steve Martin, James Earl Jones, and Penn and Teller.

DISNEY QUIZ

Who supplied the German-accented voice of Ludwig von Drake, Donald's uncle and frequent host of Disney TV shows?

Paul Frees, the same actor who gave *Adventures of Bullwinkle and Rocky* nemesis Boris Badenov his Russian accent.

NAME THAT 'TOON

In what March 1929 cartoon did Mickey Mouse dress up as a belly dancer and shimmy in drag while Minnie was visible only on a poster in the background?

"The Opry House" (Two months later, in "The Karnival Kid," it was Minnie who shook the screen as the shimmy dancer.)

About the Author

Eve Zibart is a bona fide Disney expert, having written two previous books on the subject, *The Unofficial Guide to Walt Disney World for Grown-Ups* and *Inside Disney: The Incredible Story of Walt Disney World and the Man Behind the Mouse.* She is also the restaurant critic for the *Washington Post*'s Weekend section; a regular contributor to *USAir Inflight,* the *New England Financial Journal, Impress,* and *Four Seasons* magazine; and the author of *The Ethnic Food Lover's Companion, The Eclectic Gourmet Guide to Washington, D.C.,* and *The Unofficial Guide to New Orleans.*